THE COLORED GENTLEMAN

AMS PRESS
NEW YORK

Yours Truly
D. I. Imbert

THE COLORED GENTLEMAN

A Product of

MODERN CIVILIZATION

By

D. I. IMBERT

WILLIAMS PRINTING SERVICE
New Orleans, La., U. S. A.
1931

Library of Congress Cataloging in Publication Data

Imbert, Dennis I
 The colored gentleman, a product of modern civilization.

 Reprint of the 1st ed. published by the Williams Print. Service, New Orleans in 1931.
 I. Title.
 PZ3.I313Co5 [PR6017.M38]   823'.9'12   73-18581
 ISBN 0-404-11392-3

Trim size of AMS edition of this book is 5 1/2 x 8 1/2.
Original edition is 5 1/8 x 8.

Reprinted from the edition of 1931, New Orleans
First AMS edition published in 1975
Manufactured in the United States of America

AMS PRESS INC.
NEW YORK, N. Y. 10003

Introduction

"Give me the liberty to know, to utter, and to argue freely according to conscience above all liberties." Milton.

My object in writing this story is not to criticize America nor to prejudice others against the Americans, but to record facts as I have found them, and to appeal for fairness and toleration.

Before the light of civilization that crept into the blackness of ignorance, the people of Europe and most part of Asia and Africa were in a state of hopeless savagery—they were of all shades—white, bronze and black.

It was from the East and northern part of Africa that Europe first knew the rudiments of civilization which eventually crystalized in our modern conception of well-ordered communities with all their trappings of luxuries. By a certain twist in the psychological make-up of the oriental, through perhaps environment and a difference in thought, the European civilization in time outdistanced its originator in fields of scientific development which must have been more adapted to the Western than the Oriental mind, and given more scope for research. But of all the virtues acquired by modern civilization, there is one which has not been cultivated enough so as to be extended without prejudice to an alien race—toleration.

The spirit of intolerance was carried from Europe to

the wilds of America and engendered into the hearts of the offsprings of the Mayflower Fathers. The Indians were despoiled of their possessions through banal and tricky transactions, through the offering of the Bible in one hand, and the "fiery water" in the other, which drained their robust physiques and dulled their intellect, rendering them mere puppets in the hands of their despoilers. Then later, natives of Africa were captured and brought over as slaves and treated in some instances worse than the animals in the jungles of their native land, where they lorded it and had a semblance of community life.

The lapse of time has since carried us to the maelstrom of race prejudice and unlawful excesses. Slavery, as was practiced in the Southern States will ever tarnish the escutcheon of modern civilization, it has passed, but the spirit of intolerance has not died but still thrives, even to this enlightened year of 1931.

The United States of America is a nation of cosmopolitans. There is no real American but the Indian, all residents of the United States, whether white, bronze or black, breathing the same air, helping in different ways to uphold the sovereignty of their native or adopted country, fighting its battles and paying their share to the common fund for running its government are entitled to equal protection and opportunity, to live without discrimination or prejudice, to improve their condition materially and intellectually, so that they may become better citizens and incidentally acquire a better grasp of life.

Let the foregoing and the story to follow be an appeal to all fair-minded Americans.

THE AUTHOR.

THE COLORED GENTLEMAN

I

In the living room of an elegant two-story house in the capital of one of the British West India Islands, a young man about twenty-four years old was sitting near an electric floor-lamp, reading a periodical, making notes in the margin, shaking his head in approval or disapproval as the subject pleased or displeased him. Refinement and culture were stamped on his clean-cut features, which were of an olive tint. His eyes large and lustrous were those of the idealist. His name was Francis Lafarge, the son of a successful colored merchant of the island, educated in England and admitted to the bar in London. Returning to his island home, he started the practice of his profession. He did well for three years as a limited practice in a small community would permit, but he was ambitious, and yearned for a larger field of endeavor, unlimited opportunities.

His father, a stout, elderly gentleman, inclined to baldness and wearing glasses, entered the room. Francis had stopped reading and was staring at the ceiling and wearing a bored expression.

"What's the matter, boy, in the 'dumps' again?" asked his father, "when I was your age, no one could accuse me of being a star-gazer, at least not in the heavens when there were so many brilliant ones all about me. You should be courting now instead of shutting yourself up in this room."

"That's the trouble," countered Francis. "time has changed conditions since your young manhood father, while the crampness and narrowness of life here continue. My years of sojourn in Europe which brought me in daily contact with new improvements in human life, have contributed to my somewhat restless life here. The girls are pretty and alluring enough as far as feminine charm goes, but the machinery of their intellect is clogged up by the cobweb of antiquity. It isn't their fault if they are not interesting, new ideas are slow in reaching them—they have nothing new to talk about. Nothing changes here, not even the weather. It begins to get on my nerves, and I have decided to try my luck in the United States."

At this declaration, Mr. Lafarge was visibly moved. Francis was his only son and all his hopes for the lineal continuation of his family in power and affluence were centered in him. He realized fully the aspirations of an ambitious young man as Francis and sympathized with him, knowing the smallness of his field of endeavor, given a chance, he could undoubtedly attain great heights in his chosen profession for he was endowed with much talent which required wider scope for development.

"But have you given your determination full consideration?" he asked of Francis, "do you realize what you are leaving behind?—a small country it is true, insignificant compared to the great, vast, industrial giant—America, but in this little island home, there is at least peace and happiness if not plenty of the world's wealth, pleasant associations formed from childhood, true friends and relatives whose solicitude for your welfare is genuine and sincere, a social standing and a sense of equality and importance which you could not hope to acquire in the turmoil of American life, in the aloofness in social intercourse, in the intolerance for progress of an alien race. You are leaving the free untrammeled ladder of fame and success for an existence of strife and uncertainty, an unlimited for a limited ambition for things which are only attainable by those whose only credentials are the fact that they are of pure Caucasian blood, coupled with political or financial influence. Character and integrity don't always count as dispatches in the newspapers have shown."

"It's all true and I agree with you entirely," answered Francis, "but success depends on the achievements of the individual. One must not think of failure before he undertakes an enterprise for he is sure to court disaster. I am going to try to win and with confidence in myself I think I will. Let us hope so anyway."

"So you are determined to go?" asked Mr. Lafarge, falteringly.

"I think I must, Father," answered Francis gently, "but it will be with sincere regret. You have been to me a kind and indulgent father. I appreciate all you have done for me and beg you not to doubt my love for you. I am going but I shall not forget the comfortable home and my dear ones I am leaving behind. Science you know has so revolutionized human life that distances no longer exist. With the aeroplane you could be in New York in a comparatively short time and when the television apparatus is perfected we will be able to see each other at a distance. Wonderful!"

"And the radio!" added Mr. Lafarge, "magnificent!"

"Ah! I see you also are catching the spirit of progress," laughed Francis.

"Well my boy, I understand how you feel, replied Mr. Lafarge, his hands on his son's shoulders and looking at him with affectionate pride, "You are young and belong to the new order of things—I am old, and belong to an older generation and can't visualize the future as you do. You are of age and know your own mind. I would suggest however that you write to your uncle in New Orleans of your intention. No doubt, he will be of great help to you. I understand he holds a lucrative Federal position

So it was settled that Francis was to leave for the United States.

The day of departure arrived, and he was given a good send-off by his relatives and friends. The steamer on which he was a passenger steamed down the beautiful bay protected by low green hills, out to the boundless ocean beyond, bound for the most progressive country on earth, but a democracy of capitalism and favoritism, a country where the lure of gold is uppermost in the daily routine of its citizens. The ship passed through a maze of beautiful islands that looked like emeralds on a background of silver, and on the upper deck, one could survey with great delight the placid smooth surface that stretched for miles in all directions, and in silence commune with the "Great Spirit." that is responsible for all the marvelous things we see in Nature and which we can't account for.

It was the fourth night out, while contemplating the beauty of the scene before him that an event in the life of Francis Lafarge came to pass, an event which controlled his material as well as his spiritual destiny ever after, an event which the centuries have threshed out in the course of human passion.

He had appropriated one of the deck chairs, enjoying one of the aromatic cigars one of his friends had given him on parting, and wondering if in course of scientific progress the mysteries of the planets could be solved. He reasoned to himself that it could not be possible that the Earth was the only inhabited planet, that there must be life of some sort in Mars or Venus for instance.

He was deep in thought when he suddenly looked up and beheld a vision in white, a slim medium sized figure of a young woman standing by him. She had come so quietly she almost startled him. It was as if in answer to his thoughts an inhabitant of Venus had appeared. She wore a light-weight white flannel skirt and sweater with a wide blue collar, white shoes and stockings and a silk scarf over her head. Her face was oval and her complexion fair. Her lips were full and red and her eyes shaded by long lashes shone like the stars above, but of their color, he could not tell in the light of the moon. Around her neck was a string of pearls.

Francis got up, his hat in his hand.

"Excuse me," she began, "I left a magazine on the chair you were in a while ago. Did you notice it?"

"I didn't notice anything on the chair when I sat in it, perhaps someone picked it up to read and laid it somewhere else. What magazine was it?"

"Snappy Stories."

"I have read a copy of it—very interesting. Perhaps it is somewhere about here, let's look." But the magazine could not be found.

"Never mind, I only wanted it because I don't feel like sleeping at all tonight," and she dropped into a nearby chair, "isn't it beautiful tonight!"

"Magnificent!" he replied, standing by, his hat in his hand, "it's only in the tropics one finds such glorious nights."

"And nowhere life seems so calm as on an unruffled sea," she answered, "and nowhere it is so easy going as in these islands. The people never seem to be in a hurry and always have a cheerful word for everybody. Do you belong there?"

"I am a native," he replied simply.

"Lived there all your life?"

"I was seven years in England, toured France and Italy."

"And how did you like those countries?"

"They were all delightful, and each has its own peculiar charm. For instance—England for its country-side. France, its gaiety—Italy, for its works of art."

"Is this your first trip to the States?"

"My first trip, and I hope I shall like it as well as the continental countries. I have heard and read a great deal about it and I must confess that I am very anxious to see New York, the wonder city of great cities."

"Will you please sit down. It must be tiresome standing there like that."

"Thank you," he answered simply, and he dropped into a chair next to her. Their faces were then at the same angle, and they could look at each other better. He could see by the light of the moon the purity of her matchless beauty and the little brown mole on her left cheek which he had not noticed before. She on her part kept her eyes busy taking in every detail of his expressive and interesting face.

"You may smoke if you like," she told him, "I like the smell of a good cigar, though I don't think I could take a wee puff at a cigarette. I interrupted your smoking when I came."

He took out his cigar-case and selected one, lighted it, and gave a little sigh of satisfaction as he settled back in his chair, all the while she was looking at him with a little quizical smile.

"Are you on a cruise of the islands?" he asked politely.

"Yes, one of Cook's tours through the West Indies. There are twelve of us girls, chaperoned by a lady representative of the Travelers' Aid Society."

"And your name, please, if I may ask?"

"Juanita LeBlanc."

"Pretty," he commented. "You are of French extraction, are you not?"

"My father is French from New Orleans—my mother, a Martiniquan. She died when I was a baby and I have no recollection of her. My "Mammy" told me she was a beauty of the brunette type."

"And do you live in New Orleans?"

"It's our home town. Just now my father is in Washton on some political business. But say, you are quite a cross-examiner. You've got already my whole life's history," and she gave him one of her ravishing smiles.

"And pretty history it will make before it's done, I wager."

"Is it a prophecy?"

"Almost a conviction."

"Are you a weather prophet?"

"Better at human nature and character."

She looked at him intently for a moment then said, "And I predict great things for you. What is your destination?"

"New York—eventually—New Orleans."

"Indeed!"

"Strange?"

"Did you just make up your mind for New Orleans?" she asked mischievously.

"That part of my program was settled before I left home. I have an uncle in New Orleans."

"Well, life is a merry-go-round. Here today and somewhere else tomorrow. Last year I was in Egypt and the year before in the Hawaiian Islands, two extremes. God knows where my fancy will take me next year," and she made a little grimace. She looked at her wrist-watch. "I must be going, my friends will be sending a searching party for me pretty soon," laughingly. She got up, bade him good-night and walked swiftly away to her cabin.

When she was gone, he went and leaned on the railings, looking far out on the shining sea, his mind with the girl he had just met, wondering under what circumstances he should meet her again in her country. It was late when he turned in to find his suit-case had been tampered with and some important papers stolen, and finding no clue to the intruder after reporting the matter to the officer on duty, he went to bed and it was late when he woke up the next morning.

II

Francis saw very little of Juanita the balance of the voyage. The other girls and the chaperone were always in her company. They had a few casual meetings of short duration during which she unconsciously let him see the admirable woman nature that was being developed within her, the natural process of moulding the girl into womanhood, the forming of character and the waking of the soul to a full realization of the problems of life. She listened attentively to his mature discourse on subjects pertaining to creative science, of the great wonderful inventions worked out with laborious care and incessant perseverance in the laboratories of America. With her college tutored mind, she grasped easily all the essential points of his talk and enjoyed his eloquence.

At the dock in New York, he saw her for a fleeting moment to say goodbye, and before they parted, they exchanged cards, hoping to meet perhaps in New Orleans.

He had a letter of introduction to one of his father's agents in New York who had been informed of his coming and who was to meet him at the pier. Among the papers that were stolen from his suit-case was that letter of identification. As he was looking over the rails at the crowd on the pier after the gangplank had been let down, he felt a hand on his arm, and as he turned around, a flashy dressed man was extending his hand to him, calling him by his name and welcoming him to New York. He asked him about his father, whose business relations with him he greatly appreciated. His name he gave as Mr. Hartley, member of the firm of Hartley & Son, Inc. He asked Francis for his baggage checks, promising to look after same for him and hustling him down the gangplank to a waiting sedan which after they had entered drove swiftly away.

"What hotel have you selected for me, Mr. Hartley?" asked Francis after they had rushed through the traffic of the great metropolis and racing up Fifth Avenue.

"My father and I live in a beautiful flat a few blocks from here and we thought you would feel more at home and comfortable with us than at a hotel."

"It was very thoughtful of you. Thank you very much," replied Francis.

Before an elegant six-story apartment house, the sedan stopped and Hartley and Francis got out, the former after speaking a few words to the driver ushered Francis in the vestibule where they entered a self-manipulated elevator which took them to the top floor, opposite to a door in the hall in which he inserted a key and asked Francis to enter. The room was spacious and well furnished, and after Hartley had shown him his room and the bath of which he was glad to immediately partake of, Hartley went to the phone and called up a number, and after a long, low conversation with a party on the other end, turned with a smile of satisfaction on his face, turned the key in the door and taking a magazine on the center table, flopped full length on the upholstered davenport.

In about an hour afterwards, after Francis had finished his bath and repaired to the front room, a knock was heard at the door and when Hartley opened it, a portly man of about sixty entered, and to whom Francis was introduced as Mr. Hartley, Senior.

"Glad to see you Mr. Lafarge," he began, shaking Francis' hand, "our business relations with your father have been very pleasant and lucrative to us. I understand he is interested in many concerns on the island, is he not?"

"Besides his mercantile business," answered Francis, "he is owner of an extensive sugar cane plantation, a rum distillery and agent for Lamport and Holt Steamship Co."

"Yes, I know," replied Hartley, Senior, "Dun and Bradstreet, rate him very highly. Are you his only son, Mr. Lafarge?"

"Yes, but I have a sister who looks after my father's household, my mother having died some years ago."

"I suppose he is a very indulgent father to you."

"He is one of the best of fathers."

"By the way, Mr. Lafarge, it strikes me that your father could make a lot of money here through us. A company is being formed in which my son here and I are directors to control most of the foreign-owned oil wells in Venezuela. Three-quarters of the shares are already sold in blocks of $1000.00 each. There is approximately $150,000.00 more to be disposed of and I would advise your father to take some of that, say—$50,000.00 worth. The company has a capital of five million and some of the wells according to our experts are inexhaustible—a great chance to make a lot of money—Mr. Lafarge and he took a large envelope from a safe in the wall, extracted printed shares and documents from it, reports from engineers of international fame and favorable comments on the venture from financial and commercial papers.

Francis was impressed by all the proofs of sound business basis on which the company was formed and of the known integrity of the directors. He agreed to send a cable to his father advising him to give him power to act for him and to send him a draft for $50,000.00.

In the meantime, in a room on the 30th floor of an office building in the brokerage district, another scene was being enacted.

Sitting before a large glass-top desk with papers of different colors piled on it, a stout man of forty was writing when the office boy knocked at the door and at the command to enter opened it and announced a visitor.

"Where is his card, didn't he give you one?" he asked the boy.

"No Sir, he just said to tell you a party wants to see you."

"Show him in."

When the boy faced about, the man was already at the door and pushing the boy aside entered and shut it. He strode straight across the room where the other man was sitting and with drawn pistol ordered him to stand up.

"Put on your hat and come with me," he commanded. "Tell the boy as you go out to tell your father you are going out of town on some business for a few days and to close the office. Don't make an outcry or attempt any monkey business. If you do, I'll fill you full of lead, understand that. Keep quiet and do as you are told and no harm will come to you."

They took the elevator to the ground floor and walked out to the curb where a sedan was waiting for them in which they entered.

The office boy however had become suspicious, and taking another elevator immediately after them had followed, and as the sedan was moving away, had jumped on the bumper.

The sedan stopped at the apartmenthouse on Fifth Avenue where the two men alighted and entered the house. The boy in the meantime had taken down in his notebook, the license plate number of the machine and the number of the house, and departed.

In the room on the top floor of the apartment house, the two men calling themselves Hartley, Senior and Son, were alone, having sent out Francis for a drive about the city in charge of one of their trusted agents. The son was saying—"It's a good thing you got my radio from the ship in time, for she got to her berth ahead of time."

"Yes, and I am glad you got on to that bozo, for business has been quiet here ever since you left," answered the father.

"Well, we'll have to detain Hartley here a while till our little business is finished. We'll have to get from him the key of his office, so as to intercept any message old man Lafarge may send him. He was in his office an hour ago, Martin ought to have got him by this time."

A knock was heard at the door and when the son opened it, the man called Martin and his companion entered.

"Ah, glad to see you Mr. Hartley, please sit down. I am sorry we had to resort to this action, but for good reasons we'll have to detain you here a few days. It will be a little inconvenient for you, I know, but if you do as you are told, you needn't worry."

"But it's an outrage! I don't see why you fellows should prey on respectable people like that."

"You are not going to lose anything. We are not going to ask you for any money—only your signature to certain documents."

"Hell, you'll get!"

"Profanity is not in order here, Mr. Hartley. We use

nothing but courtesy."

"Not among thieves."

"You should say—financiers, Mr. Hartley. One must possess fine business ability to accomplish all our undertakings," answered the elder man, then he went to the safe in the wall, took out some papers which he spread on the table before Hartley, prompted by a browning at his ribs.

"I will ask you to kindly put your signature to these documents, Mr. Hartley."

"What for?"

"Just as director to a big corporation."

"What the devil are you talking about?"

"Well you see, we are forming a company to take over all the small oil companies in Venezuela, and we want you as one of the directors."

"I'll be blowed, if you fellows haven't got nerve to hatch up such a scheme!"

"It requires that, in all transactions of magnitude, Mr. Hartley. Please sign."

"I won't."

"You won't?"

"No!"

"I guess you will before you are permitted to leave here. Martin, take Mr. Hartley to his room and take his keys away from him."

The next morning a cable came to the office of Hartley & Son, Inc., from the West Indies for Francis, and Martin was there to receive it. It referred to a draft of $10,000.00 as down payment on the purchase of shares in the newly formed corporation, from the elder Lafarge. The money was cabled to the branch of the Bank of Canada in New York.

About two o'clock in the afternoon, two men could be seen lurking in the doorway of a department store across from the apartment house. Presently, a sedan drew up before it and Francis with the other two men posing as Hartley & Son, appeared and got into the sedan. Immediately, the two men across the street got into another machine and followed.

The sedan drove straight to the Bank of Canada where its occupants got out and entered the bank. The other machine following them drew up also to the curb and its two occupants got out and entered the bank, one taking a position at the entrance, the other, keeping close to Francis and the two conspirators. They went to the foreign window where Francis presented his credentials and enquired about the draft which was cabled to him. The bank official said that they had received instructions to pay him the $10,000.00 on demand and would be glad to accommodate him. The money was counted over to him in ten, one thousand dollar notes. Then he, and the two other men turned to a writing stand in the middle of the bank where some papers were pushed over to him to sign and the money exchanged hands. At that moment, the man who had kept close to them all the while, pushed two pistols to their ribs and ordered them to a corner of the bank where he relieved them of their artillery and the money they had just secured.

"Say, young fellow," he addressed to Francis aside, "you don't know these two birds probably. Well they are two of the crookedest crooks in the country. You were due to lose $10,000.00 right now if it wasn't for the tip of a poor boy who played detective. He is Mr. Hartley's office boy and if I were you I'd give him a reward."

"Well, you don't say," answered Francis bewildered. "They certainly played their parts well. I never had an idea they were not what they represented themselves to be. Where can I find the boy?"

"He is now at headquarters, let's go."

They were all jammed in the police machine, the two crooks hand-cuffed together.

In the meantime the apartment house on Fifth Avenue which had been under surveillance was raided, releasing Hartley and arresting Martin who after showing fight submitted to the police.

The three of them were tried, found guilty and sent up the river for a term.

Francis, having recovered his baggage, moved to a hotel from which he emerged later in the day in the company of Mr. Hartley to have a look at the fanciful spectacle of Mammon on parade on Fifth Avenue of which he had heard and read much. In many instances he found a great similarity of color in the night life of New York and London, touched here and there with sham imitations of the delectable "insouciance" of Parisian Bohemian life, without its "naivete," chivalry and fraternity of common interest. In almost all he saw, he found an inclination in the people to outdo the world, a childish mania to have the biggest, tallest, most powerful of everything in existence, a determination to make New York the show-place of the world, yet, the average New Yorker has very little conception of the rest of the world, to him, New York is New York, and New York is the world. He knows very little of geography and cares less.

Everybody seemed to be in a hurry to catch something and even take chances with Death, such as getting on and off moving cars, standing at quick lunch counters with hat on, swallowing their food so rapidly as to invite indigestion. From morning till night, day in and day out, they toil at their calling to snatch the elusive dollar without limit, without knowing when to stop and enjoy their hard earned money.

Instead of the office, at regular working hours, the dinner table of a club is used to discuss and consummate great transactions which end sometimes in operation for appendicitis due to improper assimilation of food. Mammon rules the great American Metropolis with an iron hand, and Death daily gathers his toll of exhausted efforts.

Francis was not long in grasping the situation, and as he lingered in the Metropolis he found many opportunities to examine with a critical eye, the delicate mechanism of America's social and political life. He was astounded to find the extent of political power. He found that the voter votes by order of his employer, and the candidate makes his pantomine to the order of the "Boss"—the all-powerful in American politics. Fortunes are made and destroyed according to support given or denied. Money talks, and all are subservient to Mammon.

In Harlem, he noted the progress the negro had achieved in the short space of his forbears' emancipation which is the best answer to his fitness for universal toleration, but he also found that the colored lawyers had not the same standing in court as their white colleagues.

Visiting Ellis Island, he was surprised to note the low

standard of the immigrants that were knocking at the door of the United States for admission. In literacy and hygiene they were not any better than the negroes inhabiting the tenements in Harlem—American citizens, born and bred in the United States, speaking the same language, having the same habits as their white American countrymen, but who were discriminated against in preference to murderous Italians, and unassimilated Bulgars, Czechs, and the Tartaric people of Eastern Russia. They came burdened with inborn centuries old traditions and customs, obstinate ,and with a low estimate of the need of culture and refinement. They are admitted, and for convenience, become American citizens, but nine out of ten remain loyal to their native land and government. The public schools, for whose maintenance the colored population of the United States are made to pay in taxes for the common fund, are thrown open to the children of these European riff-raffs, while those of the negroes in many districts are inadequately provided for.

It is true that in isolated places where the blessings of modern standard of living and education have not reached the negro, where opportunity for development of character has been denied him, he still retains his primitive desires and commits crimes, but he is never the super-criminal that we read about almost every day in the newspapers. He is not the patricide, racketeer and gang-murderer we read about. The ordinary crimes he commits are also committed daily by his white American brothers, but the major crimes, the revolting ones are mostly the acts of the imported European riff-raffs.

Let the infusion of the veneer and polish of culture and refinement in the negro, and allow it full sway, untrammelled by discrimination, he will prove to be as capable as any of his white brothers as it has been proven in all walks of life all over the world.

All races have their characteristics good and bad. The good should be cultivated and the bad weeded out by degrees with patience and perseverance.

All of these things came home to Francis after a review of conditions in New York and adjacent states of which he had heard, conditions which must be changed if the United States would observe the principles of that Statue of Liberty at the entrance of its great commercial city—a statue meaning to represent in fact and in spirit what it implies—liberty. But liberty of actions, of conscience and conviction is a sham in the social and political life of America.

The United States has been governed alternately by one of its two great political parties. Unless some profit can be derived from him, has any of them been free enough and brave enough to recognize merit in the negro, to realize that he is striving for education and enlightment and should not be hampered by discrimination on account of his color?

A month passed and Francis still delayed his departure for the South, and on a morning visit to the office of Mr. Hartley, Jr., who had taken a great liking to him, he met and was introduced to a Mr. McDermott, a power in the national Republican party. He was a middle-aged, red-faced man of medium height, inclined to stoutness, with features beaming with good nature. They shook hands cordially and entered into conversation with animation. Francis was much impressed with the broad-mindedness of his new acquaintance, and on his part, Mr. McDermott was delighted with the frankness and straight-forwardness of Francis' character.

They had conversed on different subjects when their conversation turned on Prohibition.

"So you don't believe in Prohibition," mused Mr. McDermott with a smile, "and would repeal the 18th Amendment?"

"I would if I had the power and my choice."

"And be as dead as a door nail politically afterwards."

"Well that would remain to be seen."

"Being a foreigner you don't know of the powerful influence behind Prohibition, the millions invested and deriving huge profits in its name."

"Being a foreigner, I know of the illicit trade in liquor being carried on between nearby foreign ports and the United States, and which it is impossible to absolutely stop. But it is not only the smuggling that is to be eradicated. Your great problem is the one at home—the poisoned stuff that is manufactured surreptitiously in great quantities in every town and city of the Union and sold to both young and old, undermining their health and intellect and driving them into the school of crime. Three-fourths of the crimes committed now, mostly by the youths of the country can be traced to bad liquor."

"But you must bear in mind that it is only a few short years since we inaugurated the crusade against Mr. Barleycorn and we have made great progress."

"Officially, yes. In fact, no. Prohibition would be allright if it did make what it was supposed to do—stamp out liquor. Instead, it has created a spirit of rivalry among housewives as to whose homebrew is the best. It has made of the Americans, a law-breaking nation. It has made hypocrites and criminals of thousands of men receiving pay from the government to enforce the law and accepting bribes to defeat it. The cellar of the rich is well stocked with imported stuff for which he pays outrageous prices which are beyond the means of the average workingman. In spite of the army of special officers to enforce the Volstead Act, liquor is still being made, in spite of the fleet of Coast Guard boats patrolling the sea, liquor is still being smuggled. It cannot be stopped and it is a waste of money and effort."

"Good. You seem to have a legal mind."

"I am a lawyer. I studied law in England and hope to practice in this country."

"And what remedy would you suggest for Prohibition?"

"Repeal, and allow the manufacture and sale of light wine and beer under government control, but no coming back of the saloon."

"That wouldn't prevent the smuggling of whiskey, brandy and other intoxicating liquors."

"Such stuff could be kept in bond at government warehouses and sold on permit by identification. No drug stores should be allowed to sell liquor under any circumstances, and physicians should not be given license to prescribe for liquor for many unscrupulous ones through their professional status have broken the prohibition law for a fee."

"Your ideas sound good, but it would take a tremendous shuffling of the cards to put them through."

"I think it is very simple. Just put it squarely before the voters and the majority wins."

"Do you expect to locate in New York?"

"No, my final destination is New Orleans, and I expect to proceed in about a week."

"Before you leave, drop in to see me. I have a friend in New Orleans who may be of service to you," and he gave Francis his card, and departed.

III

In an elaborately furnished room of one of the stately mansions on Palmer Avenue in New Orleans, Juanita Le-Blanc was arranging some roses in a vase on the center table when the door-bell rang and she went to answer it. She looked surprised when she saw Major Reilly at the threshold.

"Why little girl, you don't look very pleased to see me. What has come over you since I saw you last?" he exclaimed as he took both her hands in his.

"Nothing, why do you ask?" coldly.

"Somehow you don't act the same as you used to. Have you fallen for another Prince Charming?"

"If I did, then what?" coquettishly.

"There would be battle between us for our lady fair."

"But in this 20th century, it's not allowed. The loser should show his mettle by being a good loser, that's all."

"For all that, I would fight for you." He took her to the davenport and made her sit down, then—"Do you know what I have come for?"

"I haven't the least idea," laughingly.

"I told you when I left, I was coming back this time for your answer."

"You must remember I am not yet through college and I cannot give what you ask serious thought," she countered.

"Yes, but will you promise?" he urged.

"I cannot promise anything, since I don't know yet my own mind on the subject."

"I have asked your father permission to press my suit with you and he has acquiesed.

"My father has my happiness at heart and will leave my matrimonial decision strictly to me, knowing full well a father cannot rule his daughter's heart. You can try to win me, it is a man's privilege, but it is up to you to succeed."

"Can't you learn to love me, as you can see I am devoted to you?"

"I have a great regard for you and perhaps that feeling may eventually turn into love. A woman's heart is something she herself can't understand. I am quite young, and Love and Marriage are two problems the heart and Destiny alone can solve. Let me be free for a year, then you shall know. In the meantime don't think anybody is going to kidnap me."

"If this is your answer, I suppose I shall have to abide by it," he said resignedly.

"Exactly, just wait. But remember, I promise nothing."

Major Reilly was a six-footer, bronzed, with sandy hair cropped close and grey eyes that looked keen. He was attached to the Aviation branch of the army and made frequent flights all over the country. He had an air of superiority about him which made those that came in contact with him dislike him. He was about thirty-five, a native of Virginia and served with distinction in the World War and was decorated with the Croix de Guerre.

The telephone rang and Juanita got up to answer it.

It was from her father, telling her not to wait for him to dinner as he had to attend a political meeting.

"I think I had better be going as I must get ready for my flight to New York in the morning, said the Major as he stood up to take his departure, "remember that I shall be thinking of you in my waking hours and dreaming of you in my sleep."

"But you must not lose your sleep keeping thinking of me too much."

"Well, I am going to mark this date in my calendar and at the end of the year, I shall remind you of it," and he pressed and held for a few seconds the soft hand that she extended to him.

It was May, the day had dawned in a wealth of sunlight when the L. and N. train from the north arrived in New Orleans with Francis aboard. He was met at the train by his uncle, an official at the United States Custom House and a staunch Republican, who escorted him to the Monteleone Hotel, where he decided to remain.

The next few weeks he employed in visiting all the interesting places in the Vieux Carre, in getting informed of all the old legends and traditions of which the city was replete. Then he applied for information regarding his citizenship which would enable him to practice, but found out he would have to wait two years before he could do so.

One day in going over his papers, he came across the letter of introduction Mr. McDermott had given him to his friend, Col. LeBlanc, and wondering if the Colonel could be the father of Juanita LeBlanc he had met on the ship to New York. He consulted the City Directory and found LeBlanc to be a common name in New Orleans. He decided to call immediately on the Colonel to settle the matter. The address was in one of the office buildings on Carondelet Street and he repaired thither. On a door on the 10th floor the name of Chas. T. LeBlanc, attorney was engraved. He went in and faced an elderly man at a typewriter who looked up and asked him what he could do for him with the suavity of the factotum.

"I should like to see Col. LeBlanc, please," answered Francis, giving him his card.

"Did you make an appointment, Sir? The Colonel is busy just now."

"You can take my card in if you please, I'll wait."

"Very well, Sir, please be seated."

Francis sat down and as the man opened the door of the inner office, he heard a voice, vibrant in tone, a voice whose owner seemed to be very much annoyed. The office man returned with the information that the Colonel would be pleased to see him. Francis crossed the room and as he entered the inner office, the Colonel was bidding goodbye to his visitor and saying—"Of course, Major, this is a matter I leave entirely to her. Hope to se eyou again soon," and then shook hands. Major Reilly passed out, looking hard at Francis.

Colonel LeBlanc held Francis' card in his hand when he turned and looked at his new visitor and by the smile on his face seemed favorably impressed. He shook hands cordially with Francis when he had read the letter of introduction from Mr. McDermott Francis had handed him.

"And how is my old friend, Mr. McDermott," he asked Francis, "Ours is a friendship that has lasted since college days. He was quarterback of our team and all the boys were proud of him. He was good at everything in college and he has made good in politics. I see by what he says you expect to locate here. Did you just arrive?"

"I have been here a month," answered Francis "and have been giving the city the 'once over.' You have a very interesting city with great possibilities if its future is entrusted in capable hands."

"Ah! that's the rub—to have capable, patriotic citizens with the welfare of the city at heart to run its government. I see by your card you are a lawyer."

"Yes, and I intend to practice here as soon as I have received my citizenship papers, which will be two years hence."

"Do you think you will like it here?"

"So far, I like it pretty well. I feel more at home here than I did in New York. It reminds me very much of my own home, with its low step houses, and balconies, and I have noted with pleasure the urbane hospitality of the inhabitants."

"We must be good to the stranger within our gates if we want others to be good to us."

"That's true, but some people don't always practice that doctrine of brotherly love so essential to the right way of living."

"Well, the world goes on, Mr. Lafarge, and we human beings are but the pawns of fate. We drift on to what purpose, we have no idea. Anyway, we must all live our life out, and the good or evil of our actions are recorded in the Great Book of Life."

"Are there any great problems to be solved in the South, Colonel?"

"One of long standing—the race question, and a new one—the Ku Klux Klan. The race problem will adjust itself when the negroes have redeemed themselves by education and thrift. When you shall have resided in the South awhile, you will notice that it is mostly in the rural districts where there is dense ignorance among the negro population and a tendency to sluggishness, that one hears of lawless excesses against the negro. In the cities where educational and occupational opportunities are more easily obtained, one seldom hears of a race problem. The Ku Klux Klan is one to be handled with extreme care. We call it new, but in reality it is as old as the race question. It is patterned a great deal after the old "Vigilantes," and I believe, as the "Vigilantes" died out, the Ku Klux Klan will follow suit."

"I am afraid however," answered Francis, "that all these periodical upheavals in the lives of nations breed distrust and animosity, and trouble to an extent we cannot foresee. In India we have the British, a handful of Europeans so to speak, trying to force their civilization on millions of Hindus of many castes and centuries old traditions and denying them autonomy. The Chinese resented the ignominy of the treaties that have rendered them vassals to the Western powers and are waking up to the possibilities of their overwhelming numerical strength. The up-to-date alert Japanese resent the restrictions against their nationals —all on account of their color, alien to the Caucasian race. Should all of these peoples combine in course of time, trained in the arts of modern warfare and determined to be recognized as equals, determined to break down forever the bars of prejudice and discrimination, what chance would the Western Powers have?"

"If anything like that should happen, it would indeed be a sad picture to contemplate."

"And yet, such a thing may come to pass, not in this decade of course, but in generations to come, if race prejudice continues."

Col. LeBlanc was a typical Southern gentleman of high stature, with mustache and imperial, a national committeeman of the Republican party which was daily gaining strength in the Crescent City.

The telephone rang and a little shrill voice came over the wire. "Of course, you can come right over, I have no particular engagement just now. I'll be here all afternoon," answered the Colonel, and he put up the receiver. He turned to Francis who had got up to go—"what do you expect to do before you obtain your citizenship papers?"

"I haven't made any plans yet."

"Come and see me some time next week, perhaps I can use you to some advantage and in the meantime you can make yourself familiar with American Judicial Procedure."

"Thank you, Colonel, I'll be glad to avail myself of the opportunity."

A little knock at the door and at the Colonel's "come in," the slim figure of Juanita LeBlanc appeared in the doorway, immacurately attired in an Alice blue Fifth Avenue model. Her complexion which was ordinarily creamy, became pink as she surveyed the room and her large hazel eyes rested on the well-built, smoothly fitted figure of Francis Lafarge, his hat in hand, ready to depart. He bowed to her as she advanced and extended her hand to him which flutterd nervously in his warm fervent grasp, while the Colonel was looking on inquiringly.

"Mr. Lafarge and I were passengers on the same boat from the West Indies to New York, papa, dear. He helped me looking for a book I never found," laughing delightfully.

"And during that search, Miss LeBlanc, I was robbed of valuable papers," and he recited to Juanita and her father the circumstances following his arrival in New York.

"Well, well, you have had some experience already haven't you?" said the Colonel, while Juanita was staring at him compassionately. He looked at his watch, then bidding them goobye, went out.

After he was gone, Colonel LeBlanc, loking affectionately at his daughter, made her sit down in a chair near his desk and said, "Now, little girl, what's on your mind? Pinched for speeding?"

"Not so bad as that," as she took off her gloves.

"Then take it off your mind."

"That's exactly what I have come for."

"What do you want—a loan?" he asked, chucking her under the chin, her two rows of ivory teeth glistening and her eyes dancing with merriment.

"You are a bad guesser, papa. I don't believe you could succeed if you were to try a hundred years."

"I give up—What is it?"

"Now listen—It is about something I have been wishing very much to do,—something that ought to have been done long ago but overlooked by those who are quite able to do it. It seems to me, it should give as much pleasure and satisfaction to the giver as to the recipient, and he or she should feel rewarded for being able to give."

"Well, well, my little girl is turning philanthropist, is it?"

"If you want to call it that, allright."

"Then what is it?"

"You know grandma left me $10,000.00 when she died, which has been accrueing interest for the last ten years. Well, I would like to buy a piece of land in Gentilly and put up a building on it for a refuge home for unfortunate negro girls who are sincere and willing to live a clean and upright life."

"Well, I declare! Do you know if you go at that rate child, by the time you are forty you shall have squandered your fortune and mine in charities," and he tried to look serious but couldn't, as he looked at the mischievous smile of his daughter, "I think I should put you back in the nursery."

"But honest papa, I am serious about this matter."

"You must have been having day-dreams."

"I have been slumming. It is interesting pastime and a help to find out existing conditions. I think it would be a good idea for the City Fathers to go slumming once in a while. They'll find plenty that will need their attention. First, the so-called Social Clubs ought to be closed, they are nothing else but gambling places, and the poolrooms are the headquarters of all sorts of crooks."

"You certainly have the experience of a social worker."

"I am one."

"And what other reform your honoress advocates?"

"Bring back the curfew to stay for boys and girls under 18."

"To hear you talk, child, one would have the impression that you are seriously interested in the moral rescue of humankind."

"So I am. Very much so."

"Then what do you propose for me to do?"

"Purchase that land in Gentilly at the best figure you can and see about the erection of a building that will accommodate forty girls."

"If you are so set on this, child, I suppose it's up to me to see about it," and he jokingly remarked, "when all your money is gone, you can call on me for an application in some old Ladies Home.

IV

Six months had swiftly passed since the arrival of Francis in New Orleans and he was now doing clerical work and studying the statute books of American Judicial Procedure, in Col. LeBlanc's office. He often met Juanita with whom he had long conversations.

"Where is papa?" She had asked him one morning as she entered the office. "I was to meet him here at ten and he is not here. Can you imagine anything more lamentable than being disappointed?"

"Oh yes," answered Francis, giving her a chair," not to be understood. A good many calamities in life happen by not being understood. If we would only try to understand one another and make allowance for the little peculiarities of human nature, there would be less cause for the breaking of ties that bind us in business . . ." and he looked at her somewhat confused.

"Finish it," she prompted,—"Love or friendship isn't that what you were trying to say?"

"Quite so. Some people are so susceptible to rashness that they rave unnecessarily if you happen to step on their toes. They don't try to realize you didn't mean it."

"In life one needs a great deal of self-restraint, especially so in politics. Believe me a man needs all that—and courage too in a political career."

"Politics must be a very fascinating game."

"It is, as long as you hold the trumps, otherwise it is discouraging to be losing on the tricks."

"And get a black eye sometimes as I hear they indulge in, in Ward politics."

"That's nothing compared to attempts to besmirch one's

character. I have a lady friend,—a Mrs. Rutledge, who dabbles in politics and it's a shame the way they abuse her in the opposition papers to discredit her."

"Well for one thing," replied Francis, "I don't approve of women in poltiics. There should be a limit to the encroachment of women in men's preserves, for the good of their own sex, and politics belong to men only. There is too much mud-slinging by certain elements which cannot be controlled, for a woman to live in that atmosphere. Even though she is not the object of attack, her association with it coarsens her nature and renders her, what you call it,— hard-boiled. What is your friend going after in politics?"

'She is trying to have the Mothers' Pension and Maternity Bills pass through the Legislature. She made a speech before that body last summer in support of those two measures. Her fine personality and masterly delivery of the subjects gained her great popularity and applause, but so far she has not succeeded in putting them through. She is very sympathetic. She is helping me with the Home in Gentilly and with her guidance and counsel the venture is beginning to bear fruit."

"When is the great opening scheduled?"

"In about a month and if you don't mind, I am going to put you on the program."

The door opened and the Colonel entered in an apparently disturbed mind.

"You are late papa. What's the matter, anything wrong?" inquired Juanita.

"Much of everything is wrong," replied the Colonel sitting down. "A delegation of property owners at Gentilly attended a meeting of the City Council this morning and lodged a protest against the erection of your philanthropic home in their neighborhood."

"I don't see what that has to do with their living where they are as the building is being erected on a tract by itself and nowhere near any white resident. But my Lord, can't a people breathe the same God-given air as others whether white or black!" exploded Juanita.

Legally, I don't see how they can prevent it. The Supreme Court has ruled against segregation of races in certain residential districts. The land is yours, you can build on it for educational purposes if you like. Surely a Home for the uplift of humanity cannot be called a nuisance."

"That's the point. I hope you made that clear to them."

"They claimed that such an institution in their immediate neighborhood will depreciate real estate values and retard improvements."

"Shucks! Why don't they attend to their bad drainage over there. Where the Home is being built is on higher ground and away from that whirlpool when it rains. I guess they are jealous of that."

"I told them we are going to finish the Home for its occupants and they can move if they like and there are plenty negroes who can buy their property on a premium."

"Good shot!" What did the Council say?"

"My political opponents, some of whom were at the meeting sided with them of course, but the Council took the matter under advisement and in my opinion will do nothing."

"Then you advise me to go ahead with my plans and pay no attention to this rabble?"

"Sure, everything will be on schedule as planned, even to the little speech this young man here will deliver at the Grand Opening," and he smiled benignly at Francis.

"What do you propose to do this evening?" Coming home early?"

"No, I have an appointment at the Choctaw Club and will dine there. Mr. Lafarge has an engagement too at Loyola, so if you don't mind, you can take him in your roadster and drop him there as it is in your direction."

"I am a nervous driver, Mr. Lafarge," she turned to Francis with her radiant smile, "you had better be sure your insurance has not lapsed for you never know what may happen."

"Well, if anything should happen and I pass out, insurance won't do me any good. I'll be buried anyway."

"And how about me?"

"In heaven, ladies are admitted free."

"So they are here,—in some places."

Having finished what he had to do, the Colonel closed his office, and the two, for the first time in their lives, took their first auto ride together. He enjoyed the new sensation of closeness to the girl who was lately uppermost in his thoughts, living in the delicious scent emanating from her exquisite person, admiring the perfect contour of her face, and the beautiful hands that guided the machine. She, bringing to memory their first meeting on board ship that glorious, moonlight night, dreaming of the days of extreme desires that ensued, and the realization of a love that was suddenly born, leaving her weak and trembling in her stateroom. Fate had been kind to them both so far, had cast them together again and none could tell what the future was to bring. Another figure flashed in the background of her mental picture, looming big in disapproval, pleading for preference, a figure insisting, almost menacing, not easily dispensed with,—the major. She liked him, appreciated his devotion, but she had come to the conclusion that it was impossible to give what he was asking— her love. Wouldn't it be better, more honorable to let him know at once than to let him live in vain hopes. It was while they were both in their eloquent silence that the roadster came into a sudden crash. A woman driving a Ford sedan had lost control of her machine, swerved, and crashed into the roadster, bruising and cutting its occupants by flying glass. A passing autoist volunteered to take them to the Touro Infirmary where on examination they were found to have suffered minor cuts and shock to their nervous systems, and though Francis' injuries were not serious, on further examination it was found one of Juanita's ankles was sprained.

The accident served as an excuse to Francis to call at the Colonel's home to enquire of Juanita's health and to send her flowers which she kept long after they were faded. They conveyed to her the sentiments of the sender, meaning in their colors—sincerity and victory. Her cheeks would flush at such times and her heart would flutter in anticipation of the day when he would think it propitious to declare his love. On the other hand, she dreaded the day when she would have to face the major and tell him that his case was hopeless. He had come to enquire about her health and had sent her flowers also when he heard of the accident. She wished he had not done that, for though she appreciated his kindness and thoughtfulness, she hated to still let him think she cared for him. She had put him off for a year, and the year was as yet some time to elapse, but her mind was already made up and was determined to let him know of her decision at the first opportunity.

Summer and Autumn had come and gone and it was February again. The city was gay with colors of the Mardi Gras, and Society was busy planning functions for the occasion. The major had been ordered to Washington hurriedly, and when he called to see Juanita before leaving she was not at home, having gone to the Gulf Coast on a visit. For some reason or other, she never had the opportunity she wanted for a private talk with him, to let him know of her decision.

Today, Juanita was home, preparing for a little soiré and feeling a bit fatigued, had stepped out on the porch for a breath of fresh air. She strolled into the garden where there was a miniature lake on whose surface lilies were blooming and two white swans swimming. There was a stone bench nearby, and she sat on it watching the movements of the swans. Presently, she heard a noise in the sky and looking up, saw a plane circling low over her house and finally landed on the Golf Links at Audubon Park, opposite.

She was till sitting on the stone bench when she heard footsteps on the gravel walk behind her and as she turned, she saw her father and Major Reilly in earnest conversation coming towards her.

"Behold Circe! Where is thy magic cup?" exclaimed the Colonel in badinage.

"At the bottom of the lake. Who will dive for it?" she replied in the same spirit.

"Sorry we left our diving suits behind, Circe. What else can we do for you?"

"Sit down and watch the fishes gambol in the water. They are having their fun like all of us."

"With your permission, can I share your bench?" interposed the major.

The Colonel excused himself on the plea of having an important letter to write.

For a while they sat looking at the fishes in the lake and admiring the graceful movements of the swans, without uttering a word. Their minds however were occupied. She was nerving herself to the ordeal before her. He was thinking how cool was her reception of him.

"What's the matter, Juanita, don't you feel well? You don't look like the girl of a few months ago. Anything wrong?"

"Nothing wrong. Just not in the mood of flippancy."

"Nobody asks you to be flippant, but you seem to be changing."

"Changing in what? Well maybe I am changing from girlhood into womanhood. My mood may be changing." She was playing with the stem of an American Beauty rose she had picked in the garden. Her big police dog came bounding up to her shoving his nose up her lap for her to rub as was her custom.

"You are a nosy dog, Nero. Now what do you want?" she told him rubbing his nose and petting him. For answer he extended a paw to the Major.

"Well I declare!" he exclaimed, "it's a general petting you want, eh, old boy?" and he rubbed his back vigorously and continued, the canine race has an exceptionally affectionate nature. If we could return good for evil as they do sometimes, the world would have been a better place to live in."

"But they don't always. You play him a dirty trick, he will remember it and growl when he sees you again. Now Nero, that's enough, lay down there and be a good dog," and he did as he was told.

"Anyway, he is quite obedient and seems to understand."

"He is pretty well trained."

"And a man must be pretty well trained to your wishes, I suppose."

"If a man wants to please, his instinct and common sense will be his guide."

"And do you think, I measure to the standard?"

"It's a hard question for me to answer."

He gazed steadily into her eyes and found no answer to his spoken queries. She returned his gaze and said, "These are fathomless wells you are looking into, Sir. The man is not born who can understand woman, the different shades and lights in her eyes speak volumes and may or may not mean anything. Just now, you are far from a guess—puzzled."

"By Jove! You are right. Woman is an enigma."

"Then why you men try to solve us? You had better take us for granted and let it go at that."

"That's the trouble. We have a positive nature and cannot take you for granted. We must be sure."

"And in the end, blunder badly."

"What brought you to the conclusion of our blundering?"

"In the first place you come in an inopportune moment, without warning. I didn't expect you, and women do not like to be taken by surprise. What brought you here—the Mardi Gras?"

"You first, and then the Mardi Gras."

"Both as an enjoyment?"

"The pleasure of being near you and to hope that I may have your answer a little sooner than you promised, and I dare hope it will be favorable."

For a moment she was silent, thinking out the best way to answer him, while he was studiously observing her undecision, then—"I must be frank with you," she commenced, "I really esteem you as a friend, but as far as matrimony is concerned, I find that my heart does not respond to your wish. I have thought it over a great deal and I know positively that it would be folly for me to marry you as I really do not love you and such a loveless union would wreck our lives."

He turned very pale as he heard from her lips the doom of his desire.

"May I ask you a question?" he asked.

"If you like."

"Has anyone come between us?"

"No one has ever spoken love to me. You are the only one."

"They may not have spoken, but may have shown it in different ways."

"I don't think you have the right to question me like that. Let's go in please."

They walked in silence to the house, deep in their

own thoughts. Ten minutes later, the Major took his leave, and somewhat fatigued and nerves unstrung, Juanita went to her room.

A box was on her dresser, and when she opened it, it was to inhale the fragrant odor of some white tulips. A card was attached to the bouquet, a name she of late was quite familiar with—it bore the compliments of Francis Lafarge. She smiled and inhaled long the delicate perfume. If the Major was about, and could have seen the deep color that suffused her face and the soft light that shone in her hazel eyes, he would have got then the right answer to his query and been initiated in the intricacies of woman nature.

V

The wheels of Destiny revolve constantly to carry an issue to a pre-conceived finality. The realization of a wish is only attained by strong personalities, forceful and masterful. The weak, devoid of energy and perseverance can only spy their goal from afar and fail to reach it with their feeble efforts. Actions are the lever that raises men to eminence and annex for them devotion.

With a mind well trained and a body attuned in perfect harmony with the ethics of a clean life, Francis found himself well established in the practice of his profession as a junior partner in the firm of LeBlanc & Lafarge, attorneys at law after five years of continual residence in the Crescent City. The Colonel was a broad-minded man, a humanitarian in character, and acknowledged only merit and integrity in a person regardless of his or her antecedents. He was quite aware that Francis was not of pure Caucasian blood—to him, it was just an accident of birth, he saw only in him the embodiment of refinement and intellectuality. His daughter was a pocket edition of that most gracious man with but one difference—while the daughter was inclined to be a bit free with her acquaintance, there was a reserve in the father which was not to be overlooked.

It was in the afternoon, one day in September after the Colonel and Francis had participated in the defense of a man who had killed on provocation, while partaking of a light luncheon at one of the downtown restaurants, that events in the life of Francis began to shape a course tending to his eventual destiny. They had selected a table away from the usual crowd that frequented the place at that hour of the day, and had ordered their repast, when a tall, handsome man of middle age appeared, and spying the Colonel, made his way towards his table.

"Why Senator where have you been spending your vacation. I haven't seen you all summer," said the Colonel, rising and shaking the Senator's hand.

"I have just returned from a trip to Europe," replied the Senator, "and believe me, from what I saw in England, particularly, we are all in the same boat of despond."

"Senator Shrewsbury, allow me to present you—Mr. Francis Lafarge, my young law partner," said the Colonel.

Francis rose, and as their hands clasped, a bond of lifetime friendship was cemented between them.

They all sat down and entered into animated conversation. The luncheon passed off very agreeably in a spirit of friendly intercourse which helped all three to understand one another's views of the things that constitute true fellowship. Before their social amenities were over, however, another figure intruded in the person of Major Reilly. He had come with a friend and selected a table near the three. He came over to make his respects to the Colonel, who invited him and his friend to join his party. He introduced the Major and his friend to the Senator and Francis, and after their black coffee entered into a conversation of world interest. The Major hinted at possible Japanese aggression in the Orient, of land concessions obtained by them in Mexico to be used for army and naval bases in case of war with the United States.

"But don't you think," remarked the Senator "that all this yellow peril talk is a myth? A nation going to war needs the sinews of war, which is gold, and Japan is a poor country to tackle such a financial giant as Uncle Sam."

"Yes," countered the Major, "but moral help goes a long way in a contest. The Government of Mexico, for political reasons may seem friendly, but from what I have heard, the people are antagonistic to all citizens of the United States."

"You mean they may side with the Japanese in case of a conflict?"

"I believe so, and I wouldn't bank too much on the loyalty of the negro population of the United States. They imagine they have their grievances on account of their being discriminated against. I don't believe they deserve any recognition at all, and education only gives them the big head."

"I think you are a little mistaken there, Major," interposed the Colonel, "race-prejudice is not as bad as some people imagine. Right here in New Orleans, there are men of color who hold positions of trust, who work side by side with their white associates, and in some instances where education has imparted a certain degree of knowledge and refinement, I have found them to be competent, reliable, and as good morally and intellectually as any white person of similar advantages. Environment goes a long way in forming character as well as a free hand in developing talent. Any kind of a handicap will seriously interfere with progress, and the negro has much to contend with since his infancy."

"I am afraid though," countered the Major, "that we may wake up some day to the realization of a coalition of the black and yellow races with their objective of world domination."

"This is a remote idea," answered the Senator, "in the first place, they are so widely scattered, organization would be an impossibility, and in the second place, outside of Japan, their equipment for carrying on such a warfare could not be obtained. Granted that the people in Washington and elsewhere forsee a war of the races, the best way to prevent it is to work out a policy of conciliation towards those people that may have a real grievance against us. They agitate for equal rights and opportunities in all affairs of public life. If they are financial partners with us in running the government they certainly are entitled to an equal voice in it. We take their money in taxes and disfranchise them. If on merit they are legible for a position of trust in the government why should they be discriminated against simply on account of their color. You can't expect a race to improve if in its effort to make the grade you are continually throwing obstacles in its way."

"I think we should take a page from the colonial history of England and apply it here. In the course of my sojourn in England and English colonies I noticed the difference of liberalism in the structure of English government to ours, which brings a conflict of ideas to my mind which on the surface challenge comparison," interposed Francis. "Favoritism is seldom indulged in. The English Government is run by the people and for the people irrespective of class. Its structure is built on merit, thereby showing centuries of efficiency. The wealth of the Government is for the masses who draw dividends from its treasury when not employed—a system which though commendable in some instances, is not applicable to the United States for the simple reason that unemployment would become a chronic ailment among the immigrant element of the nation. I much prefer the old age pension of the French. They reason that after a man is sixty years old, he has done his share of the world's work and is entitled to finish the balance of his life in the security of an annuity which is not a charity inasmuch as he himself during his working days contributed a percentage of his wages to the old age pension fund. The lamentable condition of the unemployed in this country right now calls for some kind of relief while the crisis lasts and whatever steps taken by the government for the alleviation of the situation should be made permanent. For instance, all that money spent uselessly for the enforcement of prohibition could be used for a fund to give employment to the unemployed." Francis finished his peroration in a sanguine tone as if he was pleading a case before the bar of justice. His hearers were spell-bound by his eloquence and complimented him for his logic.

The party broke up and Francis went home, feeling fortified by the frienship of Col. LeBlanc and the new one he had formed in the person of Senator Shrewsbury.

The Major on his part came to know the status of Francis in the esteem of the LeBlanc family and determined to know more of the young man who seemed to be a favorite of the Colonel—and could it be possible of Juanita also? The thought angered him, and he swore, by fair or foul means he was going to wed her.

As legal adviser and trustee of "Fairhaven," the rescue home for delinquent negro girls, Francis was in the habit of visiting the institution twice a week. It was Friday afternoon when he drove up before the Home in his blue roadster.

The Matron was at the door to receive him, apparently greatly disturbed. "Well, Mrs. Harris, how is everything," he asked as he entered.

"Not as well as I'd wish, Mr. Lafarge," she answered, a paper in her hand, "I just got this. It was pushed under the door," and she gave Francis the paper to read. It was unsigned, and threatening to destroy the building if they did not move within thirty days.

"That's the work of some hoodlum around here, Mrs. Davis. I will turn it over to the police and have the place watched. You need not fear any bodily harm. It is my opinion they just want to scare you."

"Fairhaven" was a two-story frame building of twenty rooms with spacious grounds, equipped with a laundry and bakery, presided over by the efficient Matron, Mrs. Harris, helped by three assistants whose legibility was a natural tendency to kindness. Twenty-five girls were enrolled under their supervision. Six hours were counted as a full day's work, and the inmates were paid at regular wage scales, with a nominal deduction for their room and board, making them self-supporting. A savings account was opened for every inmate at a local bank, and every Thursday and Sunday they had an afternoon off to visit their friends. There was a small auditorium attached to the main building where twice a week lectures were delivered and high class pictures shown. Girls of all creeds were admitted but none over twenty years of age. Positions with families were secured for those that were tested and found reliable and efficient after three years of service in the "Home," or married off if suitors were O. K. after rigid investigation. Such was the institution established through the philanthropy of Juanita LeBlanc for the uplift of unfortunate colored girls, and three times a week a green painted roadster drew up before the entrance and this charming young lady got out to visit her "girls," as she called them and who worshipped her.

On his occasional visits to the "Home," Francis met Juanita when least expected, and being in each other's company was a surcease to the great longing for possession which was stimulating their hearts. She wished to call him by the more intimate name—Francis, but she had still to adhere to Mr. Lafarge, which sounded too formal. Anyway the meetings afforded them great pleasure and served to keep the fires of their love burning, reaffirming his conviction of her love for him which though well guarded with woman's wiles sometimes overrode them. Being a man, he had not all the little retreats and by-ways to camouflage his feelings—all the artifices of a woman secretly in love. By themselves, his face was like an open book to her, she could tell what was passing in his mind and anticipated his words even before they were spoken, but he couldn't declare his love. He had a career to succeed in, and he was then at the beginning. He knew the Colonel, or at least thought he did. He knew that all his hopes centered in his only child—Juanita, knew of his proud ancestry and of the sort of man he would deem fit to entrust his daughter with. But he suspected that under his apparent austerity, there was a great softness of heart, a determination to override pride and obsolete family traditions for the absolute happiness of his daughter.

The Colonel however did not suspect their secret attachment and was always cordial to the young barrister.

It was six weeks after the anonymous note was left at "Fairhaven," that Francis and Juanita met again at the "Home." Christmas was close at hand and the inmates were getting things in order for an entertainment. They were all assembled in the auditorium to hear a short talk on the anniversary of the birth of the Great Redeemer, by Francis, when from the main hall, a cry of fire was heard, and in another moment a terrific explosion boomed in the kitchen scattering debris all over the spacious lawn.

A panic ensued among the girls, but by the efficient handling of the situation by Francis, order was restored.

On examination by the fire department, it was discovered that the fire was of incendiary origin, and plain clothes men were stationed to watch the building and protect its occupants.

On the advice of those friendly to the institution, another location was secured and a similar "Home" built.

VI

Acknowledging the legal ability of the new barrister who of late had been practicing with such marked success, and delighted by his brilliant oratory and perfect knowledge of the law, Senator Shrewsbury thought it possible to groom him for some public office which if secured would give him a valuable ally in the coming election for Governor. He determined then to ask Francis to run for the Legislature as a member from New Orleans. The Senator had a strong political following who did his bidding without question, and with Col. LeBlanc's influence it was quite probable that he could put his scheme through.

Francis had just finished a case in court when he met Senator Shrewsbury in the corridor.

"Well, well," exclaimed the Senator as he shook hands with Francis, "where have you been keeping yourself of late? I haven't seen you for an age."

"In my usual haunt, Senator, imbued in my law books."

"Let's go to my office if you are through with your work today," and lowering his voice, continued "after a strenuous day in court, one needs a bracer. I keep a bottle of the real goods in my office for my friends only," and he winked.

The Senator's office was in one of the office buildings in the financial district and thither the two went. In the far recess of a cabinet, the Senator reached and produced a decanter half full of a golden liquid and two glasses which he put on his desk.

"This is part of a stock I had before prohibition," said the Senator, pushing the bottle towards Francis, "help yourself of this cognac, it's fine."

They both took a "shot," wishing each other good health and prosperity.

After their imbition, they sat down and began talking politics.

"Of course, I am dry by politics but wet on conviction," the Senator opined. "Show me any of those birds born in the French Quarter of New Orleans who are not."

"Plenty of them profess they are dry though before an audience until they are blue in the face," replied Francis.

"But do you think all in the audience are 'suckers!' Nine-tenths of them know different and wish for an opportunity to offer them a bottle of good homebrew. Those of the old regular organization are made that way and it is time to let them know some of us are from Missouri."

"They are truly long enough in power, the independents should try their luck in earnest at the poll next Fall."

"They should, but they lack men of statesmanship caliber to carry them through—young, vigorous men like you for instance," and he paused abruptly.

"Well, I don't know about me. I am afraid I am not well enough known to butt in," answered Francis doubtfully.

"Nonsense. Why man, you have won most of the famous criminal cases on the calendar last Fall and Winter, and you are known all over New Orleans as one of the best criminal lawyers of the State. Suppose you try the Legislature, it's a good beginning. It should be a walk-over on our ticket."

"Who will be on the opposition side?"

"As yet, I don't know. But there is time enough for that, unless they dynamite us, we'll find a way to hi-jack them."

"And there is a lot of mud slinging in politics over here, is there not?"

"That's nothing. You just have to sling back that's all."

"But if I get mad?"

"So much the better. Your fighting spirit will be up in arms then; you'll go at it better."

"So, that's politics!"

"With a big P my son."

"I suppose there is a lot of graft in it?"

"Without it, there would be mighty little inducement."

"You are pretty frank, Senator."

"Above board," and they both laugh.

"Well, when shall I get my first lesson?"

"I'll have a talk with the Colonel about it and confer with the ward bosses, then afterwards we'll put you through your initiation."

At the next regular meeting of the New Regular organization, Francis was introduced to the members and endorsed as its candidate for the State Legislature. His platform was outlined and mailed to the supporters of the new organization.

On account of a situation created in the local political arena by powerful opposition to the New Regular candidate for governor, the voters had to be informed of the "big stick" tactics that were being brought into play. The candidate, State Senator Shrewsbury was an anti-Klansman and determined to eliminate the hooded organization from State politics, consequently the "Invisible Empire" decided to carry on a campaign of aggression against the Senator and his supporters whoever they might be. They tabulated and checked up all that were known to be in sympathy with him and his candidacy, among whom was Francis Lafarge, the young barrister and the New Regular candidate for the Legislature. They began by vaguely insinuating that he was an unknown foreigner whose origin was doubtful, and that he was not long enough in the country to hold public office.

In his public addresses, he scored the hooded organization for their unfair back-thrust attack and dared them to come in the open. He pointed out that the bulk of the American population was of foreign stock, and a good percentage of the American statesmen were of foreign birth—supermen in the Council of the Nation in shaping its destiny. He cautioned his hearers that they should not pay any attention to attacks of that kind, as pernicious and malicious. He stressed on the straightforwardness of the Senator who was running for Governor—a man quite able to give the State a wise, beneficial administration, and whose integrity was unquestioned. He scored the hooded organization's charge of his being a Catholic, claiming the right of every man to his religious convictions and that religion should be kept out of politics. He advocated an eight-hour day's work for both men and women and a minimum wage law according to locations and conditions, stressing as deplorable, the moral delinquency of girls earning inadequate wages for proper maintenance due to high cost of commodities. Laws should be enacted and enforced vigorously to combat the evils of immorality and corruption. In the end he made a plea for tolerance, for uplift of races as yet beyond the pale of high culture—a task of those that have benefitted by the light that blazed the trail of modern civilization.

It was a masterly and eloquent address, and his oratory and distinguished bearing won him the votes of many hitherto wavering voters.

The day of the election arrived. Voters were cajoled and intimidated, the votes came rolling into headquarters from all the precincts towards evening. For a time, the outcome was in the balance, but when all the returns were counted and checked, the next day, it was found that Francis was elected by a substantial majority, but not before the recounting of many missing ballots and later recovered. The Senator made a strong fight for the Governorship but lost, his opponent receiving the smallest majority a candidate for that office ever received.

Francis was the recipient of many congratulations for his victory in the face of the powerful pressure brought to bear against him, and in his office, the Senator was shaking his hand vigorously in admiration and appreciation.

"Well young man, I didn't think you could do it," he was saying to the young barrister, "you certainly hoodwinked that hooded outfit allright. How did you manage it?"

"By getting up at 4 o'clock in the morning and making the round of the industrial plants and ferry boats, distributing my cards along with a statement of my campaign program."

"But did you know who was the chief instigator in the Klan outfit?"

"No, I never knew there was a special one."

"Major Reilly is a Klansman, and for reasons best known to himself, was unsparing in his efforts to defeat you. I happened to know of his activity during the campaign through one of my supporters. I did not let you know of it at the time for fear you might get excited and spoil your efficiency. Has he any grudge against you?"

"Not that I know of."

I heard there was an understanding between him and the Colonel's daughter, only a rumor, understand, boudoir talk. I just happened to overhear my wife saying something of the sort to a lady friend, and it seems she is not as pleasant to him of late as she was, and the gossips have it that there is a rival for her hand. They mentioned a name, but I wonder—" and the Senator smiled and looked at him keenly.

"The world will have its gossips, Senator. If it is true, the Colonel's daughter has a right for a preference, and whoever he is, is a lucky personage."

The Senator looked at him shrewdly and smiled.

"By the way, Senator, a fellow came to my office a few days ago, asking me if I would consider a retaining fee of $10,000.00 a year to take care of all legal matters of the "Universal Club."

"What did you tell him?"

"Well, I suspected something wrong, some traps our opponents were laying for me, so I told him that I would think it over and to come some other time."

"I suppose you don't know what kind of a place the "Universal" is?"

"I have no idea, and I should like to know."

"It's a gambling club of course, but from what has filtered through underworld channels, I understand it's a regular dive for narcotic addicts."

"I think I shall take a walk in that district this evening and find out who the members are."

"But be careful. There are some vicious fellows living in that neighborhood who for the price of a drug will knock you senseless."

It was dark, the archlight in front of the Universal Social Club was burning bright, and one by one the members were beginning to enter. It must have been a curious assemblage inside the premises, judging by the different types of men that disappeared behind its portals. They were of different nationalities, and according to their appearance, from different walks of life.

The gambler, politician and remittance man could be

easily identified from the hard faced, nervous individuals that moved in and out of the place.

The interior of the club was furnished with a long bar at one end behind which a bartender was dispensing liquor of all kinds, identical to pre-war days. At the other end of the room, green covered tables were scattered here and there at which all kinds of games were being played.

Denizens of the underworld, white and colored began to appear on the scene from mysterious entrances, waiters were doing rushing business serving cocktails at 50 cents a glass. Many masculine laps sustained more or less weight of feminine pulchritude. It was a nightly affair right under the nose of the officer on the beat.

From his vantage point across the street, Francis could notice all the movements of the habitues of the place, and having satisfied himself of the nature of the club business, he crossed the streets. Before he had reached the entrance of the club, he was accosted by a seedy-looking individual who asked him for a match—Francis told him he had none, but the fellow, fumbling in his pocket, produced one and lighting it held it close to Francis' face, then moved swiftly away. Francis was sure that asking for the match was all a ruse, that it was someone following him and wanted to be sure of his identity.

The next morning in an office in the Post Office Building, Major Reilly was interrogating an individual.

"Are you sure you recognized the barrister and that he was about to enter the club when you met him?"

"Perfectly sure."

"And what kind of an outfit is the club?"

"Well, Major, there was a lot of red tape to get admitted in there. I was afraid I couldn't get in, but I finally came across a fellow I knew who was a member, and through his influence I was admitted last night. Apparently it's a gambling den, but something else is being carried on there with the connivance of the police, I am sure."

In the meantime, the Ward Boss in whose district the club was located, was in secret conclave with the Chief of Police.

"We can't let the club go on the way they do. They violate the city ordinance too openly, it must be stopped," the Chief was saying to the Boss.

"What's wrong with the outfit? asked the Boss.

"Wrong!" snapped the Chief, "if you were to drop in there some evening, you would have all the evidence you wanted. Of course I don't know the real object of their association, that's not my business, but they must run an orderly place or as near to it as possible. Those women are liable to squeal on them anytime they imagine they have a grievance."

"Then why don't you give them a tip?"

"I have, and I think that aviator that came from Washington claiming to be attached to the Aviation Corps is an agent of the Department of Justice, sent here to investigate such cases as the "Universal," and may get us in bad."

"Have they come across this month?"

"Regular."

"Well, give them a tip a little beforehand and make a raid on the premises, that will forestall that Washington guy. By the way, what do you think of that new barrister. member of the Legislature? I heard him at a political rally at the last election, and I tell you he is a sure spell-binder."

"Does he interfere with you?"

"So far, no. I don't know anything about him. He hasn't been here long, but he has Col. LeBlanc and Senator Shrewsbury backing him, and that is no joke."

"Then why don't you try and get him in your band wagon?"

"Can't do it. I have sized him up and found he is not a turncoat. He is one of the crusader kind, the sort that would like to get at the bottom of things and expose all our legitimate commissions."

Their talk over, the politician departed, and the Chief turned to the routine of his office.

At the "Roosevelt," a long cipher message arrived from Washington for the Major, from which he received further instructions regarding the Universal and an order to bring to justice the ring-leaders of an international gang of alien smugglers who were making the club their headquarters. He went to the Chief and showed him his credentials. The Chief was impressed and promised to do what he could.

But he was between two fires, he had to please the Ward Boss and at the same time do the bidding of the Federal Government.

He finally decided to raid the club, but he was careful to give notice to the management of his intention. All the women could not be notified to stay away, so when the place was raided, some of them were arrested for not having any visible means of support, and taken in the patrol to headquarters. Among them was a colored girl not quite eighteen, of regular features and chocolate color. Francis was at headquarters on some legal business when the wagon arrived. He questioned the girl, and according to her story he understood that she was one of the unfortunate outcasts of society through the misdeeds of others. Taken in time, she had the courage and willingness to reform, and realizing this, Francis went her bail and telephoned a number. In a short time, a colored maid arrived in a machine and took charge of the girl. On the maid's arm was a band which bore the words—"Fairhaven."

Issues are changing ever, and conditions vary according to popular demands. But in the political game, it has been proved that the outcome of a campaign hinged many a time on personal animosities with a woman at the bottom of it. The Klansman organization was beaten in the last campaign, but one of its most active members, Major Reilly was still alert to bring about the downfall of the successful candidate of which the latter was aware. From what the Senator had told him, the Major was under the impression that he was a preferred suitor for the hand of the Colonel's daughter in marriage, merely a supposition, nevertheless, strong enough an incentive to undermine Francis' character, who thought it would have been more gentlemanly on his part to come in the open and air his grievance.

While reading a paper in the lobby of the Monteleone one afternoon, a contractor whom he slightly knew accompanied by Major Reilly approached him and got into conversation with him. They both congratulated him for his recent victory at the poll. The conversation drifted into different channels, and finally shifted to the highway construction work.

"I understand," remarked the contractor as he puffed

thoughtfully at his cigar, "that you are on the Highway Committee in the Legislature. Any contracts awarded since your election?"

"I suppose they would be published if they were," replied Francis, "however I am not on the committee. You are misinformed."

"But you could use your influence in the awarding of contracts," persisted the contractor.

"My influence is limited to the needs of my office, and the responsibility rests with my ability to know that the State gets its money's worth."

"I see, you are practical and conservative."

"The signs of the Times show a new star has risen in the political firmament, and it may turn out to be an all-absorbing planet," remarked the Major jokingly.

"Your telescope must be a powerful one to have shown such a star among the millions in the firmament," answered Francis with a smile.

"By the way, Mr. Lafarge, how do you like this country?" asked the Major.

"It compares very favorably with other countries I have seen," replied Francis.

"But you haven't been here long enough to make an unbiased comparison."

"Long enough to have secured all the facts in the case."

"You have made rapid strides in your citizenship."

"The duties of American citizenship do not differ in essential to those of other civilized countries."

"Are there many Europeans in the West Indies, Mr. Lafarge."

"A great many are the descendants of European nations, but very few Americans."

"Now Mr. Lafarge, it's your turn to cross-examine us," remarked the contractor.

"If I begin," replied Francis slowly, "your genealogy will be like a book of Genesis."

"That's a good retort. Now will you be good. Can't get the best of lawyers old scout," remarked the Major.

At parting the contractor whispered to Francis, "It may be worth your while to know me better, Mr. Lafarge."

"And the Devil to pay perhaps," returned Francis bluntly.

The contractor shook his head and laughed. "Not as bad as that," he said, but the Devil sometimes is a jolly good fellow. Goodbye, hope to meet you again," and he walked briskly across the lobby, out to his parked automobile outside, leaving the Major with Francis.

"Queer old duck," remarked the Major as they were left alone, but a good sort, and you may be in need of his assistance some day—who knows?"

"If ever I do, I will remind you of this hour when you advised me, but I am of the opinion that it will be the reverse. I may be called upon to defend him—one can never tell."

The two parted friends apparently, but one had a desire for revenge burning within him, and the other had a sense of distrust of his late callers.

Francis knew quite well that all those leading questions were of some purpose. He could see they were after information of some kind, but they played the game so awkward, he could not help but see through it all.

"They didn't get anything, those two rascals," he soliloquized to himself, "and whatever they were after didn't materialize. In fact they showed me that they had no trumps to play with. Well, we'll see, they may have something up their sleeves, time will show. They are both Klansmen."

VII

The seasons and months had changed and brought with them diverse temperatures and new situations in the social and political world. Francis was forging ahead in establishing a reputation for cleverness in his profession and vigor in upholding and forwarding the rights of his constituents in the Legislature.

Juanita spent most of her time doing social work, visiting "Fairhaven," and attending little social affairs, mostly among her college chums. Tonight, Juanita was giving a little party in her garden to a few intimates to which Francis was invited.

Being alive and able to enjoy the good things of life

is a fine thing to contemplate and appreciate. The verdure of the fields, the varied colors of the fruits and flowers, the softness of the exhilarating breeze—all combine to create in one a sense of contentment and satisfaction with one's self, but the best enjoyment of life is the knowledge of having contributed to the happiness of others and the possession of a sympathetic and congenial companion.

Life is a barren waste without the sweet presence and solicitous care of a husband or wife—mated and blended in one, having all things in common, anticipating each other's desires, living for each other.

Francis was in that frame of mind when he drove up St. Charles Avenue to attend Juanita's little party. He was thinking of Juanita, of her matchless beauty, her goodness of heart and intellectual attainments. He knew for sure she was the only woman in the world for him. The allure of her charm was an incentive for greater efforts for success which he hoped would eventually give him the opportunity he craved for—to bid for her possession, to have and to hold her as his own beloved wife, to love and protect her against all the petty jealousies and inconsistencies of life. So far he had not much to complain of his treatment by those who formed his world. Life to him was like a great vista of beautiful scenery with ever changing colors.

His thoughts ran thus when he realized he had passed the Colonel's house on Palmer Avenue. He chided himself for his day dream and in returning he ran into a machine that had just crossed to the wrong side of the street. The impact demolished the other machine's fender and damaged the mechanism of its engine. The driver evidently was trying to ram him, but miscalculated the distance and was hit instead.

It was a Ford Sedan, and besides the driver there was a man in the back seat holding a colored girl apparently forcibly. In a flash Francis recognized the features of the girl he had stood bail for and sent to "Fairhaven." His own machine was not damaged save for a broken windshield He whipped out his pistol and showed a police badge he wore underneath his vest to the two occupants of the sedan, and ordered them to get out and enter his machine. With his pistol at the driver's back alongside of whom he placed the other man, while he and the girl occupied the back seat, he ordered him to drive to headquarters. On being questioned at the station, the girl volunteered the information that she was forced into the automobile while returning to "Fairhaven" on her afternoon off and subjected to indignities by the two men after she had refused to be a party in a plot to incriminate the young barrister into relations with her. It was their intention she said to keep her a prisoner until she signed an accusation to that effect. That they saw him coming up St. Charles Avenue and decided to smash him. They were locked up without bail and a charge of attempted blackmail and kidnapping was preferred against them. The girl was sent to "Fairhaven," and Francis went back to Juanita's party. When he arrived, an orchestra was playing one of the soft Hawaiian pieces in the garden which was illuminated by colored electric globes in Japanese lanterns. The guests were moving about and partaking of refreshments. Francis looked for Juanita and found her surrounded by a quartete of young admirers. "What made you so late?" she asked him when she had a chance to speak to him.

He gave as excuse of tire trouble, but he knew she wasn't satisfied with that. Tire trouble did not take that long. She had almost given him up, she told him.

"Now remember, when you are invited to a party be sure to be prompt. Tire trouble next time won't excuse you. There are plenty of taxies."

"I'll surely remember that," he answered, bowing low like a courtier of old.

He could not tell her the cause of his tardiness. He was pale and ill at ease. The charge his secret enemies were trying to fasten on him was one of the most heinous an opponent could bring against another. Of course it could be easily refuted, but the mere fact that it was attempted would find credence and antagonism in some quarters. He must at all cost prevent it from getting in the press, and made a political issue by his enemies. But who they were that dared to stoop to such infamy?

Juanita noted his pre-occupation and wondered.

Presently the Colonel came to welcome him, and two young ladies called on Juanita to settle a discussion, pertaining to the feminine gender, leaving Francis and the Colonel alone.

'A young man, fresh from a victorious political combat should not look as you do. What's the matter? Why man you look as if you had just seen a ghost," remarked the Colonel.

"Perhaps I have, Colonel—my political ghost. I would rather trust a tiger than some human beings. I should like to discuss an urgent matter with you. Can you spare me a few moments?"

"Sure. Let's go to the library, there, we shall not be disturbed."

When they got there, the Colonel dropped into an easy chair and invited Francis to another near him. Now fire away. What is it?"

Francis told him all that transpired and asked for advice.

"Well, I must say, it's a pretty rotten deal they are trying to hand you. What have the two men said?"

"They have kept silent so far."

"Were there any reporters about when you and your party reached headquarters?"

"Fortunately, there was none."

"Then I would advise you to order their release after you have tried to get them to divulge the names of the party who employed them in their nefarious enterprise. Of course it's preposterous for anyone to entertain such a thing of you, but if anyone will stoop to such a frame-up, he'll stop at nothing to gain his end."

"I am quite aware of that. It's their beginning and a very bad one at that. It's up to me to show them up."

"You may trust your friends to stand by you, and I for one will always believe and trust you."

"Thank you Colonel," answered Francis as he shook hands with the old gentleman, "it is the knowledge of such confidence that will help me to fight back with unwavering determination."

When he went back to the garden, he found Juanita occupied, entertaining her guests, but serious when she noticed him, and asked him if he had been enjoying himself.

"I have been enjoying the music—with your father, Miss LeBlanc."

"And his jokes too, I suppose. He always has a new one to spring on his friends."

"This time it was one on me. There are times in life, Miss LeBlanc when one's system needs the counteracting effect of a good joke. Do you know of one?"

"By the looks of you, I am afraid a good joke would fall short of interesting you. Did you have a nightmare last night?"

Francis thought of the strange ingenuity of woman intuition, a gift of Mother Nature to enable the gentler sex to pierce through the thoughts of the unweary male.

"I came very near having one tonight. A politician is subject to nightmares, I guess. Something happens when least expected. It's in the game. What's the program?" and he looked at the gay young people dancing on the green swath, laughing and flirting.

"The program just now, is do as they do," and she made a sweep of her hand at the merry couples.

"Then Miss LeBlanc, may I have the honor of dancing this waltz with you?" and as his arm encircled her waist and the delicate perfume of her hair reached his nostrils it was as if he had drank of a delicious nectar, invigorating, strengthening his body. He forgot his troubles, unconscious of anybody else in existence, save that at that moment, she was in his arm, warm and tender, the essence of womanly perfection.

As he was leaving before the party broke up, he asked her if he could always rely on her friendship, her trust in him and what he represented—truth and sincerity, no matter what others may say to the contrary. She extended him her hand, a plump soft hand for answer which he grasped with fervor and suppressed emotion, and as their gaze met, there was no need for a verbal answer. Fortified by that assurance, he drove back to his hotel determined to overcome his enemies.

When he went to Police Headquarters in the morning, he found some one had given all the details to reporters, one of whom was a man he had done a good turn. He took Francis aside and said: "If I were you I would employ a body-guard. From what I know about the plot against you, they mean to "put you on the spot," your life is at stake.

"Well a man in public life is bound to have enemies—men who imagine they have a grievance."

"But sometimes, it's a personal, private grudge, and in that case it is more dangerous. I am not mentioning any names, but perhaps you can think of such a man. If you do, well he is at the bottom of it all, so beware of him."

"But how did you come to know all this?"

"I happened to hear a conversation between two men a few days ago. I tried to see you to warn you but couldn't locate you."

Francis immediately got in touch with both Senator Shrewsbury and Col. LeBlanc, and through their united influence prevented the publication of the affair in one evening paper, but could not induce the other two morning papers to abstain from a write-up. It came out in a big headline—

"SERIOUS CHARGE AGAINST NEW LEGISLATURE MEMBER"

In veiled language it gave its readers an account of what purported to be blackmail, finishing with the hope it may not be true, leaving in the minds of some, a doubt of innocence.

There was nothing else for Francis to do but press for vigorous prosecution of the two men. It was a highly sensational case, and in the personnel of the defense lawyers, one could see the hand of the Ku Klux Klan.

Juanita could not help reading about the case and kept herself posted of everything that transpired. Nothing however could shake her faith in the young barrister, and in the hour of need, of faithful comfort, she tried to impress it on him in different ways. She knew through her talk with her father casually about the case, of the powerful combination lined up against him——the hooded organization and the Ward Bosses affiliated with the opposition. She knew of the Major's veiled insinuations of late, of his doubt of Francis' integrity which she had resented as unworthy of a gentleman against another. She knew of his jealousy and of his sinister influence in the council of the Ku Klux Klan.

In justice to the love which she realized she could no longer conceal, she was determined to go the limit in rescuing him from the overwhelming abyss.

The case came to trial, figuratively the trial of the newly-elected member of the Legislature for his political life. The opposition machine had worked hard in trying to dig up more sensations in Francis' life to feed the people's credulity, but his life had been too clean for them to frame-up anything that would stick. The district attorney and his assistants were able lawyers and appreciated the gravity of the case. They thought it was time to call a halt in the defaming of the character of public officials without just cause.

The courtroom was packed early with spectators eager for the scandal injected in the case. The star witness of the prosecution was put on the stand and gave testimony as to what transpired at the time she had left her aunt's house to return to "Fairhaven," and of anonymous notes received, threatening her life if she gave testimony detrimental to the defense. She went through a gruelling cross-examination by counsel for the defense who pictured her as a woman of infamous character, whose testimony could not be relied on for truth. She stuck to her story and never wavered in her accusation of the two men at the bar, of abducting her, and offering her a bribe to involve the young barrister in a statutory offense against her, and when she refused, she had been mistreated till she was about to lose consciousness in the car when it swerved at a corner on St. Charles Avenue and was struck by Francis' car.

She was followed by Francis who testified to his chance meeting with the two alleged blackmailers and abductors, who seemed to be holding the girl by force in their car. The defense counsel tried to pin him down with some leading queestions which were overruled by the judge as immaterial and irrelevant.

Their defense was of the flimsiest kind, and after the jury had been out half an hour, returned with a verdict of guilty as charged. Francis was exonerated and acclaimed, but he knew it was the beginning of a battle he had to wage with unscrupulous enemies from then on. The defendants took their sentence quite stoically and never revealed the identities of their employers, who evidently interested themselves in their behalf for shortly after they were paroled.

On his desk when he returned to his office, he found a big bouquet of American Beauties with an envelope attached on a visiting card enclosed was written in a bold feminine hand "From one whose trust in you will never fail." Strong man that he was, he almost cried with emotion, as he took those beautiful roses, symbol of American Womanhood, and pressed the rosy petals to his lips—their fragrance sweet, a reminder of the delicate beauty of the donor.

VIII

As the great pendulum of Time swung back and forth, registering with precision the age of the earth and incidentally that of every human being and all things in existence, events of great importance were happening in the life of the nation. Three years had swiftly passed and Labor Governments had assumed power in England and Mexico and radicalism was rampant in most of the continental countries. Jingoism was at the throttle of the high-powered engine of the Japanese nation. A reactionary government controlled and abetted by the financial magnates of Wall Street and Big Interests was in the saddle in the self-styled land of the brave and of the free—America.

A presidential election was near and both of the leading political parties were putting their house in order for the public searchlight which was to be turned in their direction. Last minute measures were adopted to allay the grievances of certain political factions among which was the Japanese Exclusion Act. The inhabitants of the Pacific Coast who were laboring under the delusion of Japanese control of the Golden State if they were allowed further admission on American soil instructed their representatives in Congress and Senate to vote against repeal of the law. The politicians argued that every sovereign State or country had the right to make its own laws without outside interference which was true, but the Japanese Ambassador countered that it was discrimination pure and simple. He contended that if Japan's representatives were admitted on an equal footing at world conferences, if they were made a party of great powers combination for the security of the peace of the world, he could not see why her nationals should not be given the same courtesy inasmuch as they fulfilled the requirements of the immigration authoriteis. The press and political leaders came back to show that there were in the State of California five Japanese births to one Amercan in a rural community where the families were almost the same in number, and they argued that at that rate, California would have become a Japanese province in the course of twenty-five years. They pointed to Hawaii where the economic life of the island was being absorbed by the Japanese who outnumbered the natives five to one and the real Americans, ten to one. That every Japanese in Hawaii was a trained soldier devoted to Japan and her Emperor, and if at any time there should be a war between the two nations, those would be Japanese agriculturists and merchants could be in a short time mobilized into an army of occupation, outnumbering the local garison, five to one.

From a physical standpoint the situation was alarming enough, but they did not take into consideration that though the Japanese public considered the Exclusion Act a national insult, the governing class knew well enough that a war with the United States was foredoomed to defeat. They might win a few initial successes, but could not hope for ultimate victory against a nation of such unlimited resources. Anyway the ire of the Yellow Race against the Anglo-Saxon was steadily rising and in its swiftness lay the danger.

United China under able leadership was striving to have the objectionable treaties abrogated and regain full control of Shanghai and Hong Kong. She was on the threshold of an era of peace, self-assertion, and self-esteem. She had awakened from her lethargy of centuries and accepted Western methods in co-ordination with her own, with promise of world power inconceivable of her future greatness. What the outcome of the fight on the Exclusion Act would be was as yet undecided. Meanwhile, in New Orleans, certain members of the Universal Social Club were debating means to outwit the vigilance of the authorities regarding their lucrative business of smuggling aliens from Cuba and Mexico, a great percentage of which was Japanese. At the same time, at the office of the Chief of Police another scene was being enacted.

"Do you mean to say, you can do nothing with that Universal Club?" Major Reilly was saying to the Chief. "Why man, most of the members of that outfit are active agents of the Japanese Government. I should not wonder if they have obtained important documents relating to our defense of this coast and handed them over to the Japs."

"Well, Major, that is the concern of the Department of Justice. They have their agents to look into that. My business is purely municipal, I am to see only that they don't break the city ordinances."

"But I understand that at the last meeting of the Police Commissioners they were supposed to have given you orders to close up the place."

"There you are mistaken again, Major. There was a discussion on the subject, but the city attorney raised some legal questions as to unavailableness of evidence, and as they have a charter and are conducting the place apparently within the law, even if we don't think so, we can do nothing."

"Then it is up to me to secure that evidence."

"It looks like it Major."

"Now that I think of it, do you think that outfit is getting protection from the New Regulars?"

"What makes you think so?"

"One of my agents was shadowing the big boss of the place the other day, and saw him go into Lafarge's office and didn't come out till an hour afterwards."

"Anything else?"

"Well, he was seen snooping about the place the other night, for what purpose, I am going to find out."

"I happen to know, Major, that he was requested to look after their legal interests but rejected the request. I think though, he is doing a little detective work himself and if you go about it right, you may in a round-about-way get from him the information you want."

There was a knock at the door and at the invitation of the Chief to come in, the Ward Boss in whose district the club was located entered. He surveyed the room with his eagle eyes and noticed the presence of the Major. The Chief introduced them. The Ward Boss smiled broadly at the mention of the Major's name.

"I think I have heard of you before, Major?" he said patronizingly.

"Possibly," answered the Major, stiffly, "but I don't think I have had that privilege about you."

"Well, I don't advertise my wares as some people do, Major, so my stock in trade is limited to my regular customers. The boys call me "the man in the iron mask," and he chuckled good-naturedly and continued. "By the way Chief, I have a little piece of news to tell you, a good little morsel, by Jove. Do you mind the Major?"

"Not at all, fire away. I am ready to swallow it whole."

"It's about that young barrister. Lafarge who has made such great success as a lawyer and politician."

"He seems to have acquired a great deal of popularity, for it's the second time this afternoon I've heard his name mentioned."

"Anyway, he seems to have made a hit with the ladies," answered the Ward Boss, giving a side glance at the Major, "but this doesn't refer to them though."

"Come on then," kidded the Chief, "don't leave us in suspense."

"Well it's rumored that Senator Shrewsbury is grooming Lafarge for Congressman of the 2nd District. The Senator is slated for United States Senator without opposition," answered the Ward Boss, and he smiled broadly at the Major.

"That kid must have been born under a lucky star. He seems to be getting everything he goes after."

"I should say he is. But give the devil his due. He is by a long jump, the smartest young lawyer in the State today. You've heard him talk, haven't you? By Jove I've never heard such an easy flow of language from anyone else. He is a born orator and a clever one at that. He seems to have graduated in another class, too. Dame Rumor is linking his name with that of a real American Beauty."

"You don't say!" exclaimed the Chief, grinning.

"That's what. Anyway, it's only rumor, no engagement yet. You can take it for what it's worth."

"The Major got up, bade them good-bye and strolled out.

The Ward Boss looked at him in a quizzical way as he was going out with a broad smile on his face, and burst out laughing when he slammed the door. "I heard that chap is in love with the same girl, but Lafarge beat him to it. He is not o good loser I heard and is trying some dirty tricks on the young fellow. I can't make use of Lafarge, he is not the kind that will stand in my column, but I admire his courage and straight-shooting just the same. That's why I rubbed it in on the Major just now. Gee! he looked like Old Nick himself when he was listening to my news reel. But, by Jove, he won't blacken his character if I can help it," exploded the Ward Boss banging his hairy fist on the Chief's table.

"He calls him, the half-breed," I heard.

"Well, if he is, he hasn't shown any inferiority morally or intellectually to any of his fellow lawyers. They came pretty near blackening his character in the blackmail case and might have succeeded if he hadn't by chance ran into those men before they took the girl to some remote place for torture.

"I heard the Major is looking for trouble with that Universal outfit."

"He's been pretty well shadowed, and we know he is a sleuth of the Department of Justice, posing as an aviator. Those birds at the club are paying well, ain't they? So long as we get our rake-off, what the devil do we care if they are devotees of black or white magic," and the Ward Boss brought out of his stuffed inside coat pocket a roll of twenty dollar bills which he shoved over to the Chief. "That's your share," he simply said.

Outside it was getting dark, except the glaring light that was being thrown on the pavement from the headlights of the innumerable cars that were crossing the thoroughfare. The Chief had gathered up the money and walking across the room to a window, opened it. As he did so, he heard an explosion outside and saw the demolishing of a powerful machine a few yards from headquarters.

"My God! A bomb!" he exclaimed. "I saw the man throw it."

When he and the Ward Boss reached the scene, they found the bomb had completely wrecked the engine and destroyed the forepart of the machine. The driver was hurled a few feet away apparently dead. When they turned him over, to their horror, they recognized—Francis Lafarge, barrister and member State Legislature.

"God! They've got him!" exclaimed the Ward Boss.

IX

From the far East, from the East Indian City of Benares, came a turbanned swarthy disciple of Gandhi to deliver a course of lectures on ancient philosophy and incidentally to lay before the American public the present-day condition of the East Indian people under British rule. He lectured under the auspices of the order of the United Bretheren at their meeting place which was thrown open to the public. The Indian philosopher and lecturer had a perfect knowledge of the English language which he spoke without a flaw. He stressed on the aspirations of the Indian people to govern themselves, to carry on their mode of life which was best adapted to their teachings and racial inclinations without hindrance. They were a nation of millions, he argued, the wealth of whose princes could pay off the national debt of the United States, and yet the British had usurped power to control the destiny of such a nation without any perceptible change to the better in its national life. He condemned the British for fomenting trouble and encouraging petty jealousies among the native princes so as to prevent a united movement for self-assertion to redeem the prestige they had lost among their neighbors. He expressed a conviction that a reaction was imminent in the century-old resignation of the East Indian people to British rule, but it was to be done by peaceable means, by protests, boycott of British goods, reviving old traditions that sanctified life, and teaching the young generation of their duty to their national existence. He didn't believe in force, the ultimate success of the East Indian movement for self-gov- was to be through education of the masses, and appeal for the support of the civilized world.

Half hour after the lecture, no one would have identified the well-groomed, well built, silk-hatted and frock-coated gentleman who entered the portals of the Universal Club as the same turbanned, robed East Indian philosopher and lecturer who had held the attention of his audience by his forceful speaking at the United Bretheren's meeting place. A policeman passed by and looked curiously at the gentlemanly figure clad in European fashion that crossed his vision, twisted his club through his fingers and emitted a grunt. The Bull's cranium was too thick to understand what constituted a gentleman, so he passed on without ado.

Inside the club a group of foreigners were in conference. There were Irish, Central and South Americans, Italians and Philipinos. It seemed that aside of its activity in smuggling, the Club was being made the rendezvous of several juntas of politicians plotting to regain power in their respective country. The Hindu was known to the group, as attested by the effusion of his reception. He informed his hearers that he had come to the United States for the purpose of interesting certain influential personages in the movement of self-government for India, to raise financial contribution and to appoint representatives in the principal cities of the country. He wanted to be informed of the status of certain attorneys versed in international law to handle the legal end of the movement here. He had heard of the firm of LeBlanc & Lafarge, or rather of one Francis Lafarge, connected with the firm and wanted to know if he could be recommended as a suitable attorney for his needs.

"He is the squarest and cleverest lawyer we have now practicing in the State," replied the big Boss of the place, "but Swami, I don't believe you could secure his services. He turned me down, saying he wanted legitimate business only. Furthermore, he may have English sympathies, although I think he is a radical, politically. He studied in England and was called to the bar in London. He is a clean, fearless fighter."

"Anyway, I will see him, for from your description of him, he seems to appeal to me."

"He met with a terrible accident recently and is now in a hospital. In a couple of weeksperhaps he will be well enough to receive you."

In the convalescent ward of the Hotel Dieu, Francis reclining on a chair, was reading a newspaper three months after the attempt on his life. His left arm was still bandaged up, and a pair of crutches was resting on the chair by his side, but a faint healthy color was on his face which was not marred by the explosion. The article he was reading dealt with the candidacy of one of his opponents for the Congressional seat.

A look of determination appeared on his face and his eyes blazed defiance at his enemies. He had expected this, but the fact that it happened did not make it the less tolerable at a time when he could not give active opposition. But from his bed of sickness, he began to plan his campaign to fight the agents of his powerful enemies who had meant to kill him, or at least put him out of the running. The paper did not mention any name, but gave notice that he would come out in the open in a few days to get ready for the Primary. He wondered who he could be. Presently, he heard the engine of an automobile roar and stop in front of the hospital and through the window, saw Col. LeBlanc and his daughter alight. His heart gave a bound and his right hand trembled. It was several days since they were over to see him, and he had begun to wonder at their long absence. Her visit was always a joy in his life, a pleasant event he looked forward to. She had sent him flowers and books when he was permitted to read, but she never came to see him alone, the Colonel was always with her. She was still beautiful, but there was a certain grimness and determination underlying the loveliness of her face since the news of the attempt at his life was made known to her. He could not get up when she came and shook hands with him, he could not gaze into her eyes to see the great tenderness reflected there, but he could feel the trembling hand as he grasped it and held it a while, enjoyed the faint perfume wafted from her person, enjoyed her little breezy talk and delightful laugh, now that he was on the road to recovery.

The Colonel was always solicitous for his health, always in consultation with the physician in charge about the state of his health and the time it would take for him to be on his feet again.

"But Colonel," the physician replied when he was asked the same question for the fourth time in a week, "the crutches will help his candidacy instead of injuring his chances. The public will condemn his enemies for resorting to such extreme measures to get rid of an opponent. It wasn't the work of a crank, it was the last card played by a powerful combination, determined on his elimination from local politics."

But the Colonel was blind to the great unspoken love that the young barrister was nursing for his daughter, blind to her love in return. He assumed that Francis was a likeable young man, and it was mere friendship that existed between him and his daughter. He never noticed that it was she who always reminded him to visit his young law partner at stated times and never knew of the flowers that she sent him by messenger. He did not notice how pensive she was since he was injured and how cold her reception of the Major. They were signs that an outsider could not fail to see, but the Colonel never took his daughter seriously and never dreamed of her being in love. He knew of the Major's attachment for her, but he was almost certain that he hadn't aroused in her any enthusiasm for matrimony. So while he was talking to the physician in the corridor, his daughter was entertaining the patient and enjoying doing so. Left to themselves, their conversation became personal.

"Do you hear often from your people?" she was asking.

"By every mail. The Pater seldom misses an opportunity to write though he is a very busy man, having varied businesses to attend to. My sister Emily is in France, studying music. She has a fine soprano voice and the professors think she should prepare herself for an operatic career, but the Pater will not give his O. K. I have a little snapshot of her in my watch, would you like to see it?"

"I would like to very much," she answered.

"He snapped open his finely engraved jeweled watch and inside was the picture of a beautiful girl of about sixteen, with large dreamy eyes, an expressive face and wavy hair falling in abundance on her partly bare shoulders. She was smiling and there were dimples on either cheek.

"She is delightfully cute. I should like to know her," said Juanita as she gazed admiringly at the picture, one hand holding the watch, the other resting on the arm of Francis' chair.

He looked at her with hungry eyes, his hand stole over hers and gently held it. She looked at him wonderingly, with crimson-suffused cheeks, but she didn't move her hand. She just stayed quiet and looked at him.

"Juanita, dear," he began, "I cannot keep it to myself any longer. I must tell you how I love you, and in telling you I feel relieved. I cannot say that I fought it, as it has been the great incentive in my life, without it I should have failed in the struggle I have gone through. In my wakeful dreams I have pictured you as my wife, may I hope for their realization?"

She had bent her head and snapped the watch. Softly she was crying, and the only answer she could give him then, was the pressure of his hand.

It was too public for a manifestation, so Francis contented himself by patting the soft hand he held. The Colonel was in the offing and they had to be careful, so Juanita made an atempt at dabbing her eyes and nose with her powder puff.

"You two look as if you had just come from a prayer meeting," remarked the Colonel as he took a seat in a chair opposite Francis.

"We have been hearing the angels singing and the band playing, you just missed the show," replied Juanita pleasantly.

"They must have taken me for old Nick to have stopped just as I put in an appearance," replied the Colonel.

"You needn't worry papa, you'll soon hear a tune played for your special benefit."

"I hope there will be no dischordant note in it."

"I guess not, papa, the angels are well trained. What the doctor has been telling you?"

"He doesn't think you can discard the crutches very soon, young man, but you must not mind that. I am of the opinion that they'll help your candidacy."

"You think I must take the stump in the coming primary?"

"The Primary is nearly eight weeks hence, I think by that time, you will be able to hop around a few precincts which look doubtful."

"And who have they put up against me?"

"That you can't guess, I bet," replied the Colonel with a wink at Juanita.

"Not Major Reilly. I think he is more a civilian now than an army man," replied Francis, smiling.

"What made you think the major could be induced to resign and run against you?"

"I think he is more of an investigator for the Department of Justice than an army man."

"You mean a detective?"

"Something of the sort."

"Well I declare!"

"But tell me, who is the man they are grooming for the race?"

The man is a member of the Old Regular organization, a contractor with a strong following and financially able to steal all the votes he needs to beat you, and a good friend of Major Reilly."

"I think I have met the gentleman. He savors of dishonesty. If it is he, we'll have to step lively and carefully, for I think he is one of the unscrupulous kind."

"Exactly. He is a ward politician, nothing very refined about him, but he is a power in the gang."

"All the while, Juanita was listening attentively. Being the only child of the old Colonel to whom she was greatly attached. She was aware of all the intrigues of his political life. When she was home from college she served as his private secretary and in consequence became acquainted with the ways and means of getting measures through.

"But papa, don't you think it's a dangerous proposition Fran-er, Mr. Lafarge will be going up against in his weakened condition? They nearly killed him and God knows if they may not try to finish him this time."

It was the womanly solicitude for his welfare that made her speak so. Now that he had declared his love, those words she had been longing to hear from his lips, she was fearful of his safety, fearful that at the height of her happiness, something might happen to ruin her life forever.

"You may rest assured about that girlie, they will not repeat the same tactics. It never did work twice. They'll try some other kind of ammunition. I wonder what!" replied the Colonel.

"We'll have to wait and see if they have aces up their sleeves," interrupted Francis.

"Why can't we go them one better?—cheating cheaters," remarked Juanita.

"Trouble is, I don't know how," replied Francis.

"Well this is one game I know something about. We'll put a private detective on that contractor-politician's trail, and I bet we'll get some interesting things to fight with. What do you say?"

"I say that I appoint you my campaign manager. Will you accept?"

"On a percentage of the booty?"

"It may be only the other fellow's scalp," said the Colonel laughingly." Say, young fellow, she means to manage you. If she was a man, I truly believe she would have been a first-class politician. But I am afraid she has too soft a heart. She couldn't stand all the hard knocks in politics."

"You don't know but what I could hand them would be thrillers."

"By the way, Lafarge, has Senator Shrewsbury been to see you lately?" asked the Colonel.

"He comes frequently."

"The Senator is one of the cleanest men in state politics and has countless supporters that he can throw your way. Cultivate his friendship and you will find him to be a guiding star of great magnitude."

"I appreciate all that, Colonel. I have learned the value of a staunch, seasoned supporter in the political game. But what has Major Reilly to do in local and state politics?"

"Major Reilly lived here as a civilian a good many years before the World War. He identified himself in many political campaigns in this city and was at one time Superintendent of Schools. He has a following, and the Klan of which he is a member is his strongest backer."

"And he is backing that fellow against me?"

"We must presume so from information we have obtained from our private detective bureau. They are both clansmen and naturally stick together. He is of a fine Virginia family. His father and I were classmates at college.

"He seems to have strong likes and dislikes. I wonder if he realizes the table may turn on him instead in a rather crushing way, and from what I know of his activities in certain quarters he is liable to wake up some fine morning and find himself beaten to a frazzle at his own game."

"What do you mean?"

"Well, he is playing with fire when he tackles a certain social club that I know he is aching to padlock and trying to connect me with it."

"Oh, I know. It's that Universal, isn't it? He told me once that the club was a sort of agency for foreign elements not in accord with their defacto government. He also told me that he had been to California, and from observations and other sources he had found a Japanese population of 100,000 seemingly trying to make a living in agriculture and other pursuits, but in reality entrenching themselves for the day when they will exchange their peaceful implements for rifles and cannons. He declared that within a mile or two of every railroad tunnel, every bridge, and every mountain pass, there lived a humble Japanese truck farmer or a group of them. And if the tunnels were blocked, the bridges blown up and the mountain pass filled, California would be at the mercy of an invading force, within its confines. That's what he thinks."

"Well for my part," replied Francis, I believe there is more to be feared in the spread from Mexico of the Agrarian doctrine than any Japanese invasion. The time may not be far distant when there may be a clash between the inherited rich and the producing poor who are daily getting poorer while the rich are piling up their wealth at the expense of the underpaid laborers, women especially.

The world owes every man something better than a mere living wage for sickness and death are bound to come. A man ought to be able to put by a substantial sum out of his wages for such emergencies, but if his wages are just sufficient to pay his household expenses, when he is well and strong, what has he to rely on when he is ill or death comes? I don't believe in dividing the wealth of the world equally among its inhabitants, but I would suggest that all employers should know or make themselves acquainted of the habits of their employees and should they find any of them of a squandering nature a percentage of his salary should be put in a savings bank for him for his own protection or that of his family if he has any."

"That line of talk will surely please the masses if you unload it on them during the campaign, nothing like appealing to their way of thinking if it is the right way. A few disgruntled capitalists won't matter," replied the Colonel with conviction.

Francis felt happy for having come to an understanding with Juanita and henceforth they belonged to each other. Trouble may increase and the jealousies of man may interfere, but the knowledge of their mutual love would be their guiding star.

X

A week after Francis had left the hospital, and while he was going over his mail in his office, the office boy came in with a card in his hand. "Some foreigner out here wants to see you sir."

Francis took the card and looked at it with a little frown —"Show him in," he said simply. He was still weak and unable to go about without his crutches, but he was improving fast and getting ready for the Primary.

The visitor turned out to be the East-Indian philosopher and lecturer. He introduced himself and expressed a wish that Francis' health would be restored.

"I am sorry I could not attend your lecture," Francis told him, "I am very much interested in the political struggle of your country and I hope a solution will be found to settle the controversy."

"It is the sincere hope of all true patriots," replied the East-Indian," but it seems that England labors under the delusion, that being a nation of so many castes we wouldn't be able to efficiently govern ourselves. But if those in power in England would only turn back a few pages of our history they would find there written in indelible letters, an account of the glory of our people and testified to by the ruins of the monuments all about Delhi where flourished a powerful empire whose court far surpassed in magnificence any court of its day or any succeeding era."

"It is all very true," replied Francis, "but the religious question which is the fundamental obstacle in arriving at a united front will I am afraid continue to hamper all your efforts for political emancipation. All should unite for India irrespective of caste or religion. If the princes and the masses could be taught that, then there would be light ahead to blaze the trail to victory, otherwise it is all darkness and chaos."

"I hope that in the main your sympathies are with us."

"I sympathize with all those that are fighting for the recognition of their rights and striving to attain them."

"But is there no sympathy in the American people?"

"The American loves a fighter and you can depend on a certain element of the American public for moral support, but that will avail you nothing as you must have found out. The governing classes are closely connected with the British in blood, language and custom. They have their problems of their own, colonies to govern efficiently and financial, labor and racial problems at home, and are not apt to interfere in another country's domestic affairs. Your success lies with yourselves.

"I agree in all the points of your logic, but you have no doubt noticed the effect of the disobedience movement inaugurated by our great leader Gandhi."

"In my opinion I don't believe such a movement will be of any lasting benefit to your cause. It will only create disorder and put your leaders legally in the power of the British authorities. Once your leaders are jailed the masses will soon submit and it will be the end for the present at least of all your dreams of self-government."

"Are all your people here satisfied?"

"You mean with the government?"

"I mean do they all receive the same treatment?"

"According to the Constitution and the rules of fair play, they ought to, but there are prejudices which must be eradicated, and a spirit of fellowship and good-will to all men infused in the growing generation."

Out on the street, the newsboys were calling "extra." Francis rang for his office boy and bade him to get him a paper. When he returned with it, in bold type, the headline read—

"RACE RIOT IN ALABAMA—NEGROES ARMING"

The trouble was about the insistence of the manager of a Carbon Black plant in a certain town in Alabama to continue to employ negroes in spite of the demand of the white population to fire them and replace them with white laborers. A few agitators at first, grew into a mob and they threatened violence to the negroes and destruction of their property if they did not leave the town at once.

The negroes contended they were American citizens, born and raised in that section of the country, built their homes and raised families. They were a part of the community and depended on the community's industries for their living. Where could they move to? Why should they move? They had broken no law and minded their own business. They resisted the threatened forced ejection by arming themselves.

"That is just such occurrences as this that we are fighting against,—the injustice to a race that only wants to live their own lives and the right to an equal share of the world's munificence. It's a shame to have such things happen in one of the most civilized and would-be democratic countries in the world," explained the East-Indian.

"Such things are to be deplored," answered Francis.

"There might be an excuse if they were always committed by the ignorant, the unlettered," continued the East-Indian" but they are done also by members of a secret society of intelligent, civilized men who ought to know better. They are fanning a fire of race prejudice which may develop in a conflagration difficult to cope with."

"But if you will notice, it is mostly in the remote sections of the country such things happen. You seldom hear of race riots in the large cities where the negro is of a different caliber from his country cousin. And why!—Education."

"I understand you are going to try for Congressman—Is that true?"

"My name is on the ballot for the Primary."

"Well, I wish you success. But please accept this" and he took from his coat pocket a small plush case, "as a token of my esteem. It's a talisman, long in my family and claimed to bring good luck to whomever wears it."

It was a heavy gold ring set with a large brilliant ruby and four small diamonds.

"Excuse me," Francis replied, "but I don't think I should accept such a gift from you, sir, our acquaintance being so recent."

"Well, to tell you the truth, I came here with the intention to retain your valuable services in connection with our cause here, but was dissuaded to do so for certain reasons which you will pardon me for not mentioning. I heard that you are an Oxford man and I being one also I thought it proper to take an interest in you and sue for your frienship, so you may accept the ring in a spirit of fraternity."

"As you have insisted—and done it so nobly, I will accept the ring with appreciation."

"Always wear it for I have consulted the books of the great seers of antiquity about your nativity and they have all prophesied great things for you, but you must beware of certain parties at this time of your life for ahead there is danger and malice about you. The great ruby will offset all those bad influences."

"Thanks for your fortune telling," laughed Francis," really I am interested in the psychic and if I had more time I should like to give it some study."

"It is interesting and fascinating study, I can assure you."

A knock was heard at the door, and to Francis' invitation to come in, Senator Shrewsbury stepped in as the East-Indian was bidding Francis adieu.

"Who is that fellow just stepped out?"

"The Grand Vizier of the Sultan of Turkey," laughed Francis," really Senator, he is a very interesting personage. He came to pay me his respects, being an Oxford man like myself. Now, how about the country parishes, Senator, are they falling in line?"

"Don't worry, we'll beat them to a frazzle. That bunch can resort to all the dirty tricks of the game they want, it won't do them any good. We have canvassed the precincts and have ascertained the strength of the opposition. We have not overlooked anything that will materially help our campaign."

"They have ways and means to put over one or two of their candidates but we have the support and power behind us for most of the major offices."

"Now, Senator, I must tell you, how much I appreciate your kind and valuable services in my behalf, without which I should have been eliminated from the political stage."

"That's alright son, we are comrades on the firing line and we must both try to sustain the shock of battle. We have decided on the precincts you are to make addresses and the parishes you must stump. I guess you can hop around pretty good now, can't you?"

"Oh yes, I am getting about quite well now."

"That's fine. Well, I have to go to my office to prepare a brief. You must come over sometime and sample another bottle I fished out of my cellar," and he laughed while digging Francis in the ribs with his finger.

After the Senator had gone, Francis sat musing. He thought of his great incentive in life—the love and sympathy of Juanita—an incentive which was a power for endurance, guidance and perseverance without which he couldn't have hoped to continue the struggle. Love well placed and understood brings out all that is good and valiant in a person's nature, but ambition without an incentive is like a body without a soul, it loses interest when hard-pressed, loses eagerness for ultimate success and that is why sometimes, brilliant careers end so abruptly,—they lack motive power.

Francis was determined to fight to the last, knowing he had an interested audience in Juanita, and that made all the difference in the world and it has been so ever since we can remember and will be as long as there is life.

XI

On the golf links of the Country Club where Major Reilly was a member and Juanita an invited guest, whether by skillful manoeuvre of the Major or by chance, they were thrown together, and during most of that time, the Major was determined to make the most of his opportunity. They had finished playing a twosome and were on a bench in the green swath chatting on different subjects,—Juanita always leading, sensing an inclination on his part to be sentimental. In passing, a caddie dropped a newspaper in front of them on the front page of which was a sample ballot of the Primary. The Major picked it up and said,—"By the way, I see our friend Lafarge is running for Congress. I wonder if he expects to win."

"I suppose he will try, and I guess he will put up a good fight to win."

"If good wishes will help him, yours ought to blow him pass the judges' stand a neck ahead," he said sarcastically."

"I'll be glad if he wins. He deserves it."

"I wonder if there is anything in what rumor says?"

"What?"

"That he is in love with you."

"I am not responsible for what rumor says."

"But is he?"

"You had better ask him."

"I should like to know it from you. You are the best judge in that matter. Is there an understanding between you two?"

"I don't suppose I have to take anyone in my confidence have I?"

"I want to know for I may have something to tell you."

"What could you have to tell me?"

"That I still love you and no matter if you marry me or not, you must know all about this fellow."

"Well, what about him?"

"In the first place, you know nothing about his antecedents but what he may have seen fit to tell you."

"All I know is, he is a gentleman, and that is sufficient."

"He may have the appearance of a gentleman, but will he measure up to that when I tell you some facts about him."

"You mean to say you have been investigating him? I don't suppose he is a train robber or a defamer of character," and she gave him a withering look.

"He is of mixed blood,—a West Indian Creole."

"How do you know? You must prove what you say."

"I can prove it from documents in my possession, and from what he himself told me."

"And you dared investigate his antecedents though he himself told you?"

"Well it's all fair in love and war."

"You are a fine specimen of a gentleman—nit. I am not defending him, such attack from you does not need defending."

"And knowing now what he is, would you marry him if he were to ask you?"

"If I loved him, I certainly would. But that is no business of yours. If you wanted to win my love, you should have tried some other way than fighting a man behind his back."

"I told you the truth."

"What good it has done you, if it is the truth? On the contrary it has lowered you in my estimation," and she got up, "I think we had better be going."

Two weeks before the Primary Francis was kept hopping from precinct to precinct delivering addresses to interested audiences. At one meeting a rowdy bunch tried to break it up with catcalls and creating a general disturbance. They were the paid tools of the opposition and were roughly handled by the Ward Boss' men.

Francis was brave in denouncing the Ku Klux Klan whose tactics he insisted were un-American. He pledged himself to maintain the right of every individual to his opinion and conviction, pledged himself to have laws enacted for a minimum wage scale for both men and women and an eight hour law for women. He advocated the establishment of Federal Employment Offices in all cities and towns with 25,000 population and over, free of charge to the applicants and cancelling licenses of all private ones. He advocated the maintenance of a State Home for released prisoners, penniless and homeless, where they can begin life again under new conditions, live there free of charge till suitable employment is found for them. He denounced the illegal practice of lynching which should not be tolerated in a country with statute books to proceed in any case through the regular channel of the law. He always had the sympathy of the crowd, and the Ward Boss in whose district the Universal Club was located helped him in different ways and saw to it that he got a square deal with his constituents.

The morning of the Primary dawned in a flood of sunlight. All was astir as early as six o'clock in the voting booths. Senator Shrewsbury had a Republican opponent, but he was negligible. There was no doubt of the Senator's election to the United States Senate. The fight was between the Old Regular Candidate and Francis for Congress and the opposing forces were lined up for the fray. At every corner near the booths, boosters of the opposing factions were posted with buttons and badges to entice men on their way to the poll.

In the back room of grocery stores moonshine was liberally supplied registered voters and in many instances money exchanged hands or "soft" jobs promised. The Ward Boss posted his men to see that no fraud was perpetrated in the voting booths nor undue influence forced on the voters.

Francis in his office was busy answering telephone calls from friends all day long and receiving reports from his campaign manager—Juanita and the Colonel dropped in and it was like sunshine to him to have her near in that hour of doubt and suspense. He was sure of a majority in the city, but up-country where he was not well known and unable to reach on account of his injuries, a great deal of their votes would swing to his opponent.

The day passed, and official returns began to arrive at headquarters of both parties—Senator Shrewsbury looked the picture of health and confidently expected an overwhelming majority, but it was not so with Francis. The opposition seemed to have gained considerably in the country parishes since the last returns were received.

"I am afraid," he was telling the Senator, "I am due for a good trouncing."

"You just wait for the full count and you'll see. I don't suppose it will be a landslide but it will be a sufficient margin to land you comfortably in Congress."

At the completion of all returns, it was found that two up-country ballots were missing. Francis was in the lead by a small majority but the missing ballots if found would decide the winner. A thorough search was ordered but they were not found anywhere.

A special election in the two up-country parishes was ordered to determine the issue and when the ballots were counted, it was found that the opposition candidate had received a majority of only 10, not enough to offset Francis' substantial majority of 1050 for the entire State and as there was no other candidate in the field, he was elected Congressman for the 2nd District.

At Col. LeBlanc's house that evening, covers were laid for four. Juanita was resplendent in a silver tinsel dress and four rows of pearls around her neck. Her face was flushed and her eyes sparkled with happiness. Francis, a bit pale and still limping on his crutches sat between her and her father and the Senator opposite, was the acme of good nature.

"Well young man," he unbosomed himself to Francis, "I have been chasing after you all evening but like the elusive dollar, you could not be found. I went to your hotel, they said you had gone to your club, and when I got there, I was told you had just left and they didn't know for where. I just made a pretty good guess and thought I might find you here. It's a pretty safe anchorage after the storm."

"It was a pretty close shave, allright," answered Francis, smiling.

"I guess it was! You just about nosed out. It was a mighty interesting race and we must hand it to them for spunk. Those missing ballots kept me awake nights, but I figured that if the opposition thought it best to spirit them away, they must have been overwhelmingly in your favor, so I quit worrying," he looked at Francis' hand as he raised it to adjust his necktie and noticed the sparkle of the ruby and diamonds on his finger.

"Where did you get that jewel from? I never saw you wear it before."

"Maybe its donor was right," replied Francis reflectively, "I put it on two days ago and I believe it has brought me luck."

Womanlike, Juanita was immediately interested and inquisitive, "Let me see it please," she asked him in an undertone, "who gave it to you?" and she turned the battery of her beautiful eyes full at him. He smiled goodnaturedly, sensing a bit of jealousy in the question. "The East-Indian lecturer who was here two weeks ago, paid me a visit at my office claiming fraternity for being an Oxford man like myself, and made me a present of this ring. He said it was a talisman in his family and whoever wore it would be lucky. I just took it for granted, that's all. But do you know that I think there was more behind his coming here than simply to lecture. There is a movement on foot in Asia, a social and political movement far reaching in its scope, and this East-Indian visitor is one of the leaders I believe. His itinerary includes all the principal cities of North and South America." At that juncture of their conversation, the Senator who had been talking with the Colonel joined them.

"Well, what are you two plotting about?"

"Mr. Lafarge was trying to scare me with the yellow peril, but he is just kidding," laughingly answered Juanita.

"What Yellow Peril?" asked the Senator.

"I was just informing Miss LeBlanc of a few facts that may come to pass."

"Probable facts?"

"I was telling her about my East-Indian visitor and what we may expect from his visit. You know, the people of the East are restless and sensitive of their subjugation by their Western conquerors and were it not for their inability to concentrate their forces under one head, they would have tried long ago to wrest world's leadership from the European Powers. With modern weapons plus efficiency equivalent to the wonderful achievements of Japan, the millions of India and China could with a certain measure of success challenge the lordship of Britain over India and secure for China her supreme and unfettered sovereignty. What is needed now is a drive for toleration of all alien races, bringing all, high and low to the same plane of equality and fraternity."

"But you know of that little word—"if", answered the Senator, "well that's it—if!"

"I know it means a lot of things left out. But we don't get anywhere if we don't take a chance."

Juanita excused herself and went in the garden to cut some flowers.

The Senator looked appraisingly at her as she left them and turning to Francis, said. "Fine girl. You are talking about taking a chance, why don't you?"

"What do you mean?"

"Oh come on, you know well what I mean. But I don't think there would be taking any chances, for the road is strewn with roses with the thorns already clipped."

"You talk in enigmas, Senator," replied Francis laughingly."

"To be more explicit, the Colonel told me to tell you he wants to see you in his library. Go now and make the best of your opportunity."

Francis went, and found the Colonel writing at his desk. At his entrance, the Colonel closed the desk and invited him to a seat, his left hand pulling at his imperial,—a sign of concentration. He looked at him severely, he thought, but presently he smiled and extended his right hand to him saying—I must have been blind not to have noticed what was going on right under my nose. Really I never suspected the true situation if Major Reilly had not called my attention to it by informing me of certain facts about you that I knew already. He came to me two weeks ago with some documents, and he handed to Francis the papers which at a glance he recognized as the ones stolen from his suitcase on the steamer from the West Indies and among which was his birth certificate.

"How did he come in possession of these?" Francis asked with emotion.

"From a man who was sent up the River in New York for a bunco stunt on you. I suppose you can refresh your memory about this affair. Well, the man was here during the Primary and knowing of the Major's antagonism against you, approached him and for a sum disposed of these papers. He however was given 24 hours yesterday by the police to get out of town and warned to stay out. The Major came to me with these as proof of his contention to prevent a matrimonial alliance between my daughter and you."

"Have you told Miss LeBlanc about it?"

"Not yet, but I want to show you something first," and he went to a small safe in the wall which he opened and extracted a long envelope. Returning, he handed it to Francis to read. Opening it, Francis saw a photograph of a beautiful young lady of the brunette type whose features were a reproduction of Juanita's. In the envelope was also her certificate of marriage with Col. LeBlanc of New Orleans written in French at Fort de France, Island of Martinique, French West Indies and Juanita's birth certificate, also written in French, and showing Fort de France as her birthplace.

"So you see, my dear boy, she is the same as you. You are both of mixed blood, but equally superior morally and intellectually to most of pure Caucasian ancestry."

"Does she know it?"

"Yes, I have not let her be ignorant of it."

"How did you happen to go to Martinique Colonel, may I ask?"

"I was out there as American Consul and I met my wife at a ball given in honor of the officers of an American squadron. She was of a good and respectable family. We both fell in love with each other and married. She has been dead a good many years, but I have remained true to her memory."

"Will you then approve of our marriage, Colonel?"

"Is there an understanding between you two?"

"I have the honor to say your daughter reciprocates my love for her, Colonel."

"Then I suppose it's allright with me," and he shook hands with Francis, but he continued. "The wedding cannot take place right away. I will announce your engagement and when the doctors pronounce you well and able to give up your crutches, we will fix a date for the wedding."

"That suits me, Colonel, thanks.

In the Colonel's study that night, he and Juanita had a heart-to-heart talk. The bond of affection and kinship between father and daughter is one of the most sacred and indissoluble links in human life. His love was centered in his only child and daughter and on her part having not known the love of no other parent but his, lived for him and appreciated him. So when the Colonel had given his approval to her wedding with Francis, she made him promise to live with them the rest of his life.

XII

Meanwhile notable inventions had evolutionized human life in all its phases: A great percentage of the food of the new generation was of synthetic origin. Interior construction of houses was of lacquer of various designs and colors. Every radio was equipped with a television apparatus, and the airship was the only mode of travel and transport. Gas was not used but motors were operated by compressed air. The air was divided into traffic lanes and policed by air patrols. The wireless was so well developed that in conjunction with powerful telescopes on the Andes and the Himalayas, communication with Mars and the Moon was a matter of a few years perfection of the means at hand. Money, the root of all evils, greed, robbery, and murder, the incentive for war, was being advocated abolished, and a system of universal exchange put in operation, eliminating both wealth and poverty.

But the races had not yet settled their differences and smouldering fire of prejudice was still being fanned by the fanatical excesses in the red letter year of 1950. The radical government of France was succeeded by a dictatorship. Germany had annexed what was left of the great Austrian empire and once more rattling her sword. England with her far-flung empire was shaken to its foundation by the declaration of independence by Canada and Austrlia and a well organized revolt in India.

In the United States, Congress was in hot debate as to the answer to Japan's ultimatum over the Exclusion Law, and the confiscation of all Japanese properties bought in the United States under fictitious names. The Progressive Democrats were in power and threatening to disfranchise the negroes of the Middle Southern States for voting in bloc the Repulican ticket at the last election. Goaded also by late excesses of the Klansmen, the negroes were in a state of great agitation.

A league named "The Humanitarian Peace League" was launched by a few progressive and peace loving gentlemen of the South, of which Francis Lafarge, Congressman and

Chas. W. Shrewsbury, U. S. Senator were members. They and others of the League, North and South, East and West covered the United States in a campaign of peaceful education, exhorting their audiences to consider the rights of their neighbors and to treat one another as members of the human family.

While all these peace gestures were being indulged in, rumors were afloat of the awakening of the Great Chinese Dragon, and that its immense army was being secretly officered by Japanese mititary men of exceptional ability. It was even considered probable that part of that army which wast last heard of as being in the province of Mongolia had its objective in India to help in the movement of Asia for the Asiatics. At Nanking and Canton, thousands of bomber planes were being turned out from the great Government airports, and a new deadly gas invented by a European educated Chinaman with more devastating power than any yet invented.

The Soviet Government with its hordes was also in the offing, menacing, grim in its determination to pounce on any detached territory.

A division of Japanese battleships, cruisers and destroyers convoyed by bomber planes of powerful dimensions, under pretext of a world cruise was manoeuvring in the vicinity of the Philippines, and a flotilla of airships was cruising in Hawaiian waters.

All these were disturbing elements to the peace of the world, and the Chancellories of the great powers were working overtime trying to find a solution to the dreaded problem of unrest which like a thunderbolt had struck the world so swiftly. They were like the bathers unmindful of the steady and rapid rise of the tide, far out from shore and unable to race back and escape the engulfing billows. The verdict of the numerically stronger races was against them and the day of reckoning was at hand.

In Washington, Congress had rejected by a good majority the repeal of the Exclusion law but allowed ownership of land by Japanese who had been in the United States seven years and had taken full citizenship papers. However, this concession did not seem to allay the grievances of Japan who had insisted on repeal. Disagreements followed overtures by the United States Government, and insulting cartoons began to appear in the Japanese papers regarding high officials of U. S. War and Navy departments, calling them chair warmers and showing members of the Senate and Congress with half full bottles of moonshine under their coat tails.

Francis and Juanita had just returned from a long visit to his home in the West Indies where he enjoyed once more the serene calmness of life in the tropics, where great groves of coconuts with their tall trunks and wide green foliaged tops form a canopy of regal splendor,—where nature provides so bountifully to the natives of the soil,—where luxury crazed adulations have not turned into a science of egotism.

It was evening, the sun was about to set after a day of sweltering heat. Francis and Juanita with their young son Francis junior, were sitting on their front porch on Palmer avenue when the echo of a gun was heard several times in succession. He wondered what it was all about.

The telephone rang, and he went in to answer the party on the wire. When he returned, his face was pale and an anxious look was in his eyes as he turned them on his adored wife and young son.

"Juanita, dear, the inevitable has happened. Japan has declared war on the United States. A Japanese army which has been concentrating near the border in the vicinity of Tiajuana and adjacent towns in Mexico under the guise of farmers, crossed over and captured San Diego. and the Government Naval Base. They were aided by powerful bomber planes which suddenly appeared in the harbor, put out of commission, most of the naval crafts stationed there and threatened to destroy the city if they didn't surrender."

"Those dead heads in Washington ought to have perceived all that if they didn't come to a compromise," remarked Juanita.

"And what's more, the Mexicans seem to be in sympathy with them, giving them moral help, and in this they are backed by some of the Central and South American countries which had condemned the present day interpretation of the Monroe Doctrine by those in power at Washington. They resented American interefernce in their affairs which they considered unethical and tyrannical."

"I hope they confine their fighting to California and leave us alone here," answered Juanita.

"Well in these days of airial navigation a fleet of powerful bombers can soon arrive here and pulverize us in a mighty short time. Their airial outfit is superior in number and personnel to ours."

The little boy was three years old and ignorant of what was transpiring in his country, and curiously enough was at that moment marching up and down the porch with a little wooden rifle his father had given him, on his shoulder.

Francis looked at him and sighed. It was such little fellows as that, grown into manhood that pay the penalty of their country's misdeeds,—heroes, every one of them, but unrewarded for their great deeds.

"I don't see why a few men in office should have the power to plunge the country into such sufferings," Juanita soliloquized." War is not necessary to adjust national misunderstanding."

"That's true. War is the remnant of past generations handed down to us to eliminate in our new conception of life. It is the savage in man which has bred distrust of his brother, greed for his possessions, and a desire for his extermination. All these have to be revised and adjusted to fit in the new broad-minded civilization which calls for toleration and love for our fellowmen. The big stick of the cave man is a thing of the Past, so should be all weapons of war."

The League of Nations which was meant as an intermediary in all disputes among nations, and its impartial decision adhered to, could not be appealed to as the United States would not accept membership though sponsored by its own president. The Kellogg Pact had been scrapped as unworkable, and status quo in world politics was similar to that of pre-war days, viz—private pacts and alliances.

A newsboy was passing in the street crying extra. Francis bought a paper, and learned that the latest war news was that the Japanese had overrun the Imperial Valley and were making their way to Los Angeles through Riverside and Redlands, destroying orange groves and laying waste the country in their path.

The Californians rose "en masse" against the Japanese invaders. Veterans of the world War and Spanish American War were pressed into service, but not with the same enthusiasm they displayed before. The treatment they received after the World War was still fresh in their memory when thousands of shell-shocked, disabled men, deserving of compensation were left uncared for, while thousands of grafters and profiteers made rich by their sacrifices were living in luxury and plenty,—sometimes indicted to satisfy public opinion but seldom punished.

A landing was effected at San Pedro from the various battleships stationed there, but that unit was only on the defensive and dared not go beyond the protection of their ships' guns. The air battles were likewise defensive as far as the Americans were concerned. The small garrison at the Presidio, San Francisco, was inadequate to cope with the situation and unable to extend any help to the Los Angeles sector. All mountain passes and tunnels were blocked, and bridges destroyed by the enemy, isolating the state from the East and North. Mexicans, Hindus and other nationalities had flocked to the banner of the Japanese operating in Southern California, augmenting their number alarmingly, hard to control against excesses, unmindful of discipline. The women were in a state of terror at the approach of that motley crowd.

But true to their traditions, the colored population remained loyal to the country of their birth, despite ignominies and unequal treatment they received from their white countrymen. They did not take advantage of their country's difficulties and make common cause with its enemies. They performed their duties as citizens and helped to repel the invaders. After two weeks of hostilities, the beautiful city of Los Angeles and adjacent towns with all their natural and artificial wealth fell into the hands of the Japanese, and the Metropolitan city of San Francisco, guarded by its shore batteries, aircrafts and innumerable battleships in its magnificent harbor, was making a determined stand against the attacks of the enemy who used promiscuously the new deadly gas invented by the European educated Chinaman.

The Japanese carried their operations to the Panama

Canal Zone and bombed naval stores. Two battleships and a cruiser of the reserve Atlantic division were torpedoed as they were going through the canal, suspending navigation through the waterway.

The hundred thousand Japanese in the Hawaiian islands, nearly all soldiers, had seized the territory against the feeble defense of the American troops stationed there, and converted it into a naval base, thereby cutting off the Philippines from the United States.

Despite the alertness and vigilance of the naval authorities, Japanese transports were able to land large bodies of troops at different points in California and keeping their armies supplied with ammunition and equipments. The southern barrier was wide open, and a constant stream of supplies poured into the Imperial Valley for the army of occupation.

All sorts of vices were licensed and in full swing at the border towns, putting huge sums of money in the Japanese war chest.

Through the encroachment of mass machinery production of recent years, employment was steadily decreasing and the jobless absorbed with alacrity the doctrine of the Mexican Agrarian element that entered the United States in the wake of the Japanese invasion, disrupting the pacific conduct of Labor.

The commerce between New Orleans and the Pacific Coast was stopped both by land and sea, and families depending on the earnings of their sea-faring men were rendered destitute.

Such were conditions after a year of hostilities when one night at two o'clock in the morning several loud reports were heard in the vicinity of the Naval base at Algiers and a terrible bombardment ensued. A squadron of Japanese bombers had quietly crept over the city and engaged a number of American planes in battle. Bombs were dropping and exploding all over the city setting it on fire and doing considerable damage to property.

Under the command of Major Reilly, a powerful squadron of American battle planes finally appeared on the scene, engaged the enemy in a terrific air battle, destroying a number of their planes and making their commander prisoner after he had jumped in a parachute from his burning airship. But just over the river at an elevation of about 1000 feet, two planes were engaged in a death struggle. The American plane was manoeuvering to get a position on top of its adversary which was trying to aim a shot at some vital spot of its rival. The air rent with sounds of the powerful engines of the two planes so expertly handled.

Shots were fired in rapid succession but missed their marks as the planes plunged or soared high out of reach. Finally, the Japanese came close enough to fire a broadside at the American, a wing of which was shot away and its engine hit as it nosed downward and fell in the river. In it was the squadron's commander—Major Reilly of the Aviation Corps, late agent of the Dept. of Justice. The river was dragged and the plane recovered but the body of the Major was never found.

The City was under martial law. All social clubs, poolrooms and places of great gathering were closed. The Universal Social Club was padlocked and its members confined in the house of detention for the Federal authorities to deal with. Spies were plentiful under different disguise and the curfew was rigidly enforced.

From the three corners of the British Empire, India, Canada and Australia came wireless reports of rebel successes and that the backbone of British world dominion was at last broken.

Finally hostilities in the United States had come to an end with the understanding that the question at issue was to be settled at a general conference in Paris where also England and its belligerent colonies were to meet and sign the birth certificates of three new nations.

The signs of the Times were in indellible ink on the wall, but they had not heeded that the day of reckoning was near, that the era of prejudice and sense of superiority was passing rapidly that in all walks of life, efficiency and merit were the only recognized standard of true manhood and womanhood. Class as an adjunct to society was being abolished, nobility stripped of its deluded highness, and intolerance frowned upon as a sign of taking one self too much for granted. It was good for humanity that all men were not alike, their way of thinking differed and their intellect broadened or narrowed as environment and natural tendencies sway them for good or for evil. The world was like a deck of cards that had been shuffled too often, the corners were bent and frayed, a new deck was necessary and a new deal by a new dealer. The players were all getting to be experts and it was dangerous to spring any old tricks or try new ones, and so the supposed inferior races were getting into their own,—members of the same human family with equal rights and opportunities.

At the conference table of the United States and Japan, it was agreed that the Asiatic Exclusion Law was to be repealed, concessions in China abolished, and no sphere of influence allowed. Every country was to exercise its sovereign right to every foot of its integral domain, consequently all countries that illegally held any land concession in any others of sovereign class, were to relinquish such land to its rightful owner. All people irrespective of color or origin that had not attained full development were to be helped to a state of efficiency and refinement and when attained, respected and honored.

The cards were now new, face up, and the kings and queens of different suits were all alike in their bright appearance any of which could be trumps.

Francis, happily married to his mate, understanding each other, living for each other, and the little boy that was the natural result of their union, was glad that after all, there were noble souls in the world, who having made mistakes were ready to acknowledge them and willing to rectify them.

There certainly were corrupt men in high places, enjoying the confidence of the nation, but these as a rule were found out and weeded out. But there were also men of high ideals and fine morals, men that would not stoop to the petty prejudices that cram the heads of those with insufficient brains.

He was glad to realize that nearly all that he fought for and advocated were being put into practice. The League of Nations was worldwide and of international origin, but his Humanitarian Peace League was more of a heart appeal, more human in principle. It survived all attacks and helped to reorganize the New South on broader lines.

In spirit we should all try to walk in the path of righteousness, to take for our model the beautiful life of the Holy Man of Judea in which we shall find consolation and the satisfaction to know that our efforts for good have not been in vain.

All things can be adjusted, and human passion can be subdued or appeased if there is an ounce of reason left in individuals. Nations are human, not machine made, and have conscience like any individual, and as a rule the good prevails.

The signs of the Times are written on the wall, the tide of reason and tolerance is rising and whatever our sphere of influence shall be after death, we should promote by benevolent deeds on earth.

The laws of the land in its statute books are enacted for the benefit and guidance of all, irrespective of class or color and a fair trial, an impartial verdict should be accorded to all before the bar of justice.

And in New Orleans there are representative colored men of high repute and culture, leaders of their race forging ahead in their particular line of endeavor in the cause of obtaining fairness and a square deal for their race in all matters pertaining to the civic and political life of the community of which they form part—gentlemen of undoubted integrity such as may be found among any advanced group of the Caucasian race, who have risen above the difficulties of discrimination and prejudice simply on account of their color but who have all the attributes of the intelligent American citizen, some of whose names and photographs are appended in a supplement to this volume.

The End.

SUPPLEMENT

Prominent Leaders of the Colored Race in New Orleans

Who Have Achieved Success

S. W. GREEN
Businessman, civic and political leader; organizer and charter member Pride of Tonsas Lodge No. 21. Supreme Chancelor Knights of Pythias of North America and Canada, and member of several other lodges. An able and genial gentleman.

GEO. LABAT
Civic leader, Pres. N. O. Branch National Ass'n for the Advancement of Colored People, Pres. San Jacinto Club, Dist. Supt. Liberty Ind. Life Ins. Co., originator of the Registration law in State of Louisiana, member of several fraternal societies and a gentleman of honor and proved integrity.

ARNOLD L. MOSS

Senior partner Geddes & Moss Undertakers and Embalmers with a capital of over $100,000.00; Pres. N. O. Civic League, N. O. Hospital Ass'n; Pres. LaFuneral Directors, and active worker in developing Straight College, a prime promoter for the success of N. O. Carnival and member of several fraternal societies.

EMILE LABAT

A true type of the successful businessman through honesty and affability, with penetrating vision and personal initiative. Mr. Labat has built up a splendid Undertaking and Embalming business, has the respect and confidence of the community. Mr. Labat is still a young man.

JOS. A. HARDIN, M. D.
Graduate Flint Goodrich Medical College. Organizer Colored Y. M. C. A. Civic and Political Leader Indefatigable Community Chest Worker. Prime Promoter in Establishing the V. C. Jones School, Chairman Federation of Civic League N. O. and President 7th Ward League.

JOS. P. GEDDES
Undertaker and Embalmer, Pres. Colored Business League, member of several fraternal societies and active worker in all civic and political matters pertaining to the uplift of the Race. A gentleman of proved ability and integrity.

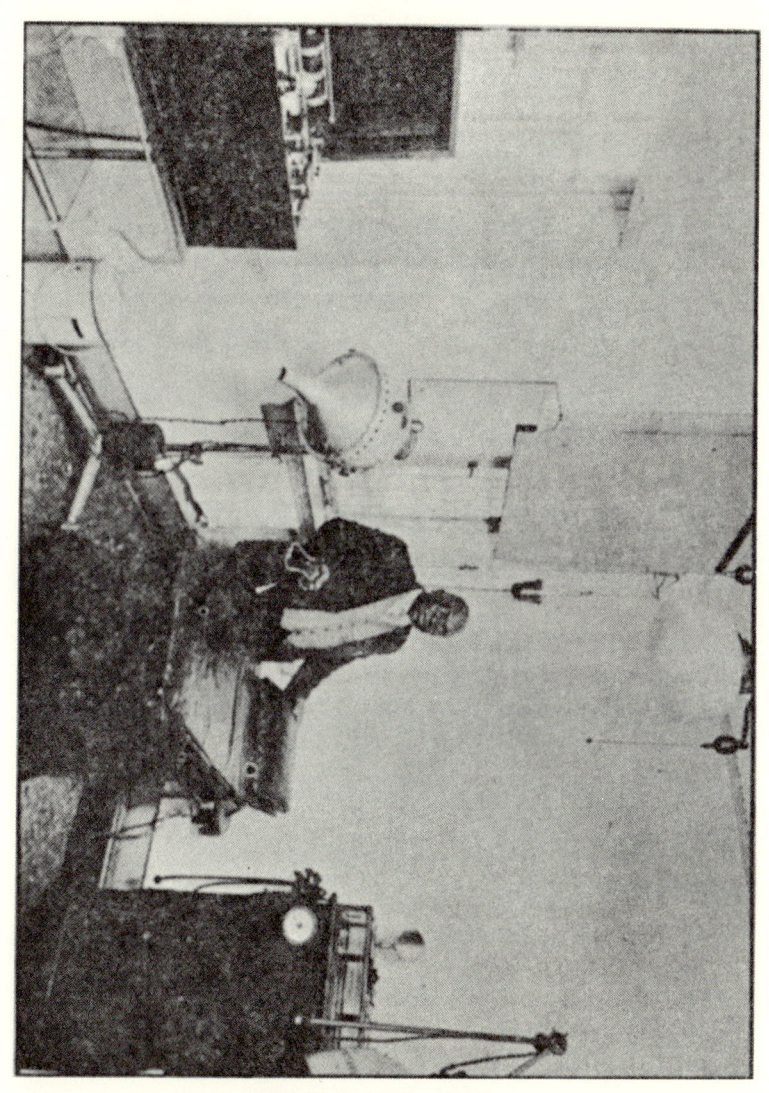

A. W. BRAZIER M. D.

Practicing physician with offices at 1104 Tulane Ave., corner S. Rampart St., devoting special attention to all kinds of disease which may be cured or relieved by electro. Theraphy or medical electricity. A member of several fraternal societies, a 33rd degree Mason, a sincere Race man and civic worker, serving on several inter-racial committiees. Pres. N. O. Medical, Dental and Pharmaceutical Assn. The above cut shows him in his office.

E. D. VERRETT

Founder and organizer Crescent Undertaking and Embalming Co. and Crescent Aid & Burial Society. Pilgrim Rest Baptist Church. Grand Treasurer St. John's Grand Lodge A. F. & A. M. Imperial Grand Treas. Ancient Arabic order of Mystic Shrine. Patron of Deborah Chapter No. 69 O. E. C. Past Chancellor Commander of Banner Lodge K. of P. and member of other fraternal societies. A gentleman who has the interest of his Race at heart.

W. H. MITCHELL, JR.

Executive Secretary Dryades Street Branch Y. M. C. A. Member Community Chest. Leader in educational and fraternal circles. Mr. Mitchell is a charming gentleman, a staunch worker for the uplift of the Race.

JAS. E. GAYLE

Graduate Straight College. Prominent in civic, fraternal and political circles. Building Supt. of Pythian Temple; Director Liberty Ind. Life Ins. Co., Secretary Southern News Pub., Co., and author of "Nils Queen Pageant."

GEO. W. LUCAS, M. D.

Late member of the Natl. Board of Directors and late Pres. N. O. Branch N. A. A. C. P., a leader in civic, religious and political circles. Late Deputy Grand Master and Treasurer, Gen'l United Supreme Council of Scottish Rites Masons of U. S. A. and Canada. Grand Medical Director Mt. Olive Grand Chapter O. E. S. and member of Knights of Pythias and Odd Fellows. Married Miss Frances A. Nesby, member of one of the best Creole families of New Roads, La.

RAOUL J. LLOPIS

Member of Carr and Llopis, Undertakers and Embalmers. A civic worker and member of several fraternal organizations. Honest and prompt in all business dealings.

List of professional and business meembers of the Colored Race in New Orleans who are helping in its material and intellectual development.

ROBT. G. WILLIAMS
Manager Williams Printing Service
A Young Man of Initiative and Vision Who Through Efficiency, Honesty and Integrity Is Building Up a Wonderful Patronage in His Printing Business. Mr. Williams Is the Printer of This Book and Does Excellent Work.

DENTISTS

Andrew E. McDonald, D.D.S., 1932 Dumaine St.
E. J. Devore, D.D.S., 2237 Dryades St.
Geo. B. Talbert, D.D.S., 2252 Dryades St.
A. J. Young, D.D.S., 1900 Jackson Ave.
J. Segue, D.D.S., 2232 Dryades St.

PHYSICIANS

Thaddeus Taylor, 1900 Jackson Ave.

DRUGGISTS

C. A. Guichard, 841 N. Claiborne Ave.
E. J. LaBranche, 1633 Orleans Ave.

SCHOOL PRINCIPALS

Thomy Lafon School.
J. W. Hoffman School.
McDonogh No. 36 School.
McDonogh No. 35 School.
Straight College.
Geo. Longe, Albert Wilbert School.
F. C. Williams, V. C. Jones School.
M. D. Coghill, Craig School.

PUBLIC SCHOOL TEACHERS

Miss R. Perkins, B. A. Hoffman School.
A. L. Speaker, B. A. Hoffman School.
Leon B. Vignes, B. A. Hoffman School.
O. C. W. Taylor, B. A. Hoffman School.
Morris A. Lewis, B. A. Hoffman School.
H. J. Cazenave, B. A. Hoffman School.
Lucille E. Bandridge, B. A. Hoffman School.
W. T. Meade Grant, Jr., B. A. Hoffman School.
Maude R. Dedeaux, B. A. Hoffman School.
Marie A. Bruce, Craig School.
Dorethea M. Earl, teacher Thomy Lafon School.
E. M. Coleman, teacher Straight College.
Miss E. V. Baranco, teacher Albert Wilbert School.

LIBRARIANS

Anita L. Johnson, Librarian Dryades Branch.
Dora E. Guichard, Assistant Dryades Branch.

INSURANCE COMPANIES' OFFICIALS

A. M. Truedeau, Mgr. Safety Ins. & Burial Beneficiaries.
Geo. A. Simon, Agt. La. Ind. Life Ins. Assn.
S. Sazon, Mgr. Standard Ind. Life Ins. Assn.

LAWYERS

F. B. Smith, 308 Pythian Temple.